Reviewers say about *The Many Faces of Friendship*:

"The well-told story of a committed life—a life of faith, a life facing difficulty (the author's daughter died and then her husband), a life which was enriched by a wide circle of friends."—THE CHAPLAIN.

"Eileen Guder's thesis: 'Life is made up of relationships. . . . They are the essence of life, and when there are no relationships that matter, all that is left is meaningless.' The author shows how friends act out the kind of service Jesus asked of his friends. She considers the difference that friends have made in her life and the characteristics of a good friend. In her usual way, the author does not succumb to sentimentality, but gives honest, forthright observations of life as she finds it. Excellent for church libraries."—PROVIDENT BOOK REVIEWS.

"The entire book is glorious reading! Eileen Guder deals with sorrow and frustrations as well as 'abundant life.' For someone who needs a fresh outlook on life, give this! Chapter 4 on 'What Money Can't Buy' is worth the purchase price that permits you to open the pages to this book and also open some new pages to your own life."—TOME TALKS BY JAMES BUSWELL.

"All the sermons by pastors from the pulpit do not have the force that human lives do, expressing Christian concern that friendship brings. . . . This is a book about friendships as experienced within the Christian family. The author tells how she and her husband were buttressed with real Christian friendships, a source of help and pleasure in helping them to be made more pleasing to God. . . . There are some sermon ideas here that would be valuable to any congregation, . . . and it is a book that will help you, through self-examination, to contribute to the witness of the Church."—LUTHERAN WITNESS.

"Eileen Guder does a good job of telling that friendship is a state of love and letting people be themselves and accepting them *as they are*. . . . This book would be an excellent addition to the ALCW and library to fit in with the theme 'The Christian in Society.' "—AUGSBURG PUBLISHING HOUSE BOOK NEWSLETTER.

"The Christian community needs a book of this character. Pastors will have opportunity to see their pastoral responsibility in the light of the experiences of this Christian family. The Christian Church will have occasion to examine its ministry to those who deeply need the kind of friendship called for in the life of its members. Highly recommended." —KDCR-FM Radio (Dordt College, Sioux Center, Iowa.)

"Out of her own experience with those who were friends with her and her husband, Eileen Guder writes crisply and perceptively of the real meaning of Christian friendship. If you enjoy learning painlessly but honestly from other people's personal experiences, you will like *Many Faces*."—THE MORAVIAN.

"With depth of understanding Eileen Guder leads the reader through the frustrations of a life focused on material things to the unbound joys of Christian friendship and its many characteristics. This book is a joy to read and a thrill to share."—THE BAPTIST STANDARD.

THE MANY FACES OF FRIENDSHIP

Eileen L. Guder

WORD BOOKS

Waco, Texas

For the many friends,
of whom only a few
are named in this book—
and especially for
Opal

FOREWORD

Life is made up of relationships. They may change and fluctuate, grow stronger or suffer attrition; be distant, or casual, even irritating. But they are the essence of life, and when there are no relationships that matter, all that is left is meaningless.

Looking back, I realize that events which altered my life did so because of the persons involved. Events *are* people— they happened because of the thoughts and actions of a number of persons. The truth of any happening, then, is partly how it affects both those involved and those who are spectators.

In a very real sense we are all caught up in series after series of happenings, whether we realize it or not. We happen to each other because we rub off on each other. Our attitudes and moods, our very silences and postures, communicate something about ourselves. The communication may be warped because we are often at odds with God; or it may be as chilly as death because of our utter detachment; but it can be healing and cheerful too. Whether we know it or not, just by *being* we are making irrevocable alterations in the lives of everyone we touch.

This is a book about friendship, and the unordinary men and women who make up the history of our lives.

CONTENTS

THE
MANY
FACES
OF
FRIENDSHIP

I

FRIENDS
INTRODUCED
US

AFTER seven years of marriage, Russ and I were impelled—or compelled—to look for something real in life because all of our goals were as distant as ever.

We wanted to get ahead in the world. Russ wanted to succeed in his profession and make a lot of money. A product of the depression who had had a harder time than most, Russ's ultimate security was money. This goal had been dimmed somewhat by his experiences during World War II, when he came to realize that his family meant more to him than just getting lots of money. But old ways of thinking die slowly, and the idea that financial success would help bring some of

The Many Faces Of Friendship

the good things of life was still a potent motivation for Russ.

I wanted those things, too—but for different reasons. All through school I had smarted under the humiliation of hand-me-down clothes, no spending money, sack lunches instead of cafeteria lunches at school, and a general feeling of deprivation. We were not poverty stricken—not at all. My father was a real estate and insurance man, and we always had enough. But the "enough" we had was pretty drab. I wanted pretty clothes, a lovely home—I wanted *things*.

When the war ended, we moved to Los Angeles because business opportunities would be better here, Russ thought. He was beginning to be a bit discouraged about getting ahead; it was slower than he thought it ought to be. I was frustrated and continually aggravated because my wants were far, far beyond our income. Shabby furniture and bargain-basement shopping were a continual irritant.

I've heard lots of testimonies to the effect that, having gotten every material *thing* one wanted in life, the ensuing emptiness drove one to Christ. Not so with Russ and me. It was many years after we had embarked on the Christian life before we began to be cured of our preoccupation with "things." We were driven to look for something—some quality of life—better than we had because we needed friends. Although we didn't realize it then, nor for a long time afterwards, our need for meaningful relationships was even deeper and more compelling than our desire for material success.

After seven years of marriage, we did have friends. Usually they were couples we met through business, and almost invariably the relationships were based on a mutual liking for the same sort of entertainment. We did things together. Now that I look back on it, I can remember very few conversations

14

we had with any of those couples that ever got below the surface of living. It was all very stimulating at times, very exciting occasionally, and—in the end—unsatisfactory. Neither of us was interested in, nor good at, small talk. And small talk is *the* communication level of most casual friendships. We were constantly on the periphery of whatever group we found ourselves in, because there were others who were funnier, and more witty, and far more adept at fielding the conversational ball. The constant effort to appear at our best was very wearing, and in the end it drove us to do something definite about discovering a more satisfying life.

For most of our marriage we had been very distant from the church, although we were Christians. By that I mean that each of us had made a profession of faith in Christ. We had been sincere in declaring our faith but it remained embryonic. The "cares and worries" of this life which Jesus warned his disciples about had gotten the major portion of our attention. It was not until these frustrations, combined with the lack of genuine friendships, forced us to face the fact that we were unhappy and without resources ourselves, that we considered going to church.

As we sat in a rather depressed state one spring evening, we heard Dr. Louis H. Evans give the regular Sunday night radio sermon from the Hollywood Presbyterian Church. "Now there's a man I could listen to!" Russ said. Next Sunday, all hopeful expectation, we went to the church. It was very large, and we felt lost and lonely in that huge congregation. Perhaps that lostness and loneliness was written very plainly on our faces, because as we left the church, a motherly woman came up to us and asked us whether we had ever attended a Sunday school class there.

To me, Sunday school classes had usually been dreary

affairs, and it had been years since we had attended anything of the sort. But we were both so desperate for some kind of reality in our lives, some people whose friendship went beyond the superficial, that we were ready to try anything. She told us there was a group of married couples our age called Homebuilders, that they met at 9:30 each Sunday morning, and how to find the classroom.

The next week we were there, outwardly very calm but inside half expectant, half armored against disappointment. I'll never forget that first Sunday morning. There was something—what, we could not have said—so different, so appealing, about the group, that we wanted passionately to be a part of it. We were greeted and introduced, and people were friendly—but that was all. And that wasn't enough. We sensed that in order to find out what made this group different in every way from any other group we had ever known, we would have to get inside. We wanted friends, and we wanted the kind of friends these people were. But would they accept us?

The whole attempt to find a new life might have died right at that point. We went to a class party, and for us it was a fiasco. It was held outdoors, because the late spring nights were warm. There was swimming, and we dutifully went swimming. Laughing and splashing in the pool, we could fancy ourselves part of the group, but the illusion dissolved when we climbed out. We were our separate selves again, waiting hopefully to be spoken to, to be drawn inside.

Later, I sat in a hammock with two other women. Neither greeted me and one of them talked on and on, in a complaining sort of voice, about how terrible it was that she didn't know anybody in the class any more, there were so many strangers. I felt myself shrinking and wished I could simply dissolve rather than be such an object of distaste. Who those women were I have no idea. Their faces and names have passed into oblivion.

Perhaps there was a sort of stubbornness about both of us, however, because we kept going. The lessons were stimulating and our need was great. It was at that time that we met three other couples who were fairly new in the class. They recognized our loneliness and invited us over. That was the beginning of a new life that happened *because* of people—and *through* people.

We met other couples and made other friends. We found that there were many new people just as lonely as we had been, and we began to be aware of the needs of others. The Christian life was just beginning to blossom in us after a long, long time of dormancy. In finding friends, we were rediscovering our faith.

It was not that the truths of our faith—the overwhelming fact of God's coming to us in Jesus Christ with its implications—weren't important. They were. But we didn't get the truth just through sermons, although they helped; nor only through Sunday school lessons, although they were the means by which we grew and learned. We didn't get it through testimonies, of which there were many. I've forgotten them all, there was nothing to make me remember. What made all the sermons and Sunday school lessons real and believable was that for the first time we had friends who really believed and lived their faith.

It was friendship that brought us in, carried us along, motivated us to study the Bible and get together in groups to talk about what we were learning. What was going on among us *was,* although none of us thought of it that way, Christianity in action.

The Many Faces Of Friendship

We were drawn into the Christian life by an openhearted friendship. It was simply a giving of themselves to us by people who did so because they loved Jesus enough to take seriously his teaching about loving their neighbor. We had nothing to offer. We were preoccupied with ourselves, restless and self-seeking, supersensitive and ready to draw back quickly if we were offended. There was no reason, really, for anyone to welcome us so warmly, other than their love for Christ which saw us as the neighbors who needed them.

It is that kind of friendship this book is about. Such friendship is the only kind that is durable enough for all the hard knocks, painful disappointments and sorrows of life. And whenever it is found outside the formal Christian community, you can be sure that God is at work there, too. He is far more generous than we think him to be, and he is at work in the world in many ways. Although this book is about friendship as experienced within the Christian family, I do not want to imply that I think that is the only place it is found. God conveys his love and grace in many ways, and through many channels. He has given us the supreme and ultimate revelation of himself in Jesus Christ, but we are never permitted the arrogance of claiming that we know everything, or have everything, of him.

After coming to know Christ many of us can look back and see how he was concerned with our lives all along. The sometimes slow process toward recognition of Jesus as the answer to life's ultimate questions is often spurred on by God's influence through many people not yet perfectly his.

II

SHINING UP MY GOOD WORKS

THE GROUP of Christians Russ and I had come into was a knowledgeable one, and we soon acquired a superficial grasp of doctrine. We could talk glibly about the grace of God, and how salvation was a free gift, unearned, unmerited. But all the time I was silently congratulating myself on having been astute enough to understand this. How marvelous it was that, out of all the people who hear the truth and fail to comprehend it, *I* had been sensitive and perceptive enough to see that God loved me and freely gave his Son so that I might be reconciled to him!

All the while I was talking about the grace of God I was

subtly cherishing my own "works," the good works of believing rightly. I had begun the life of faith in the usual lopsided fashion, heavily overweighted on the side of righteousness, not too well balanced on the scales by grace. Oh, not my own righteousness—I knew well enough *that* was sadly lacking. But in my zeal to embrace the whole of the Christian faith I came to believe there was virtue in merely believing in Jesus Christ.

The idea that there is great merit in simply believing the gospel came to me quite naturally by a superficial reading of the New Testament. Jesus' words, for instance, when the crowd asked him what they should do to carry out the work of God and he replied, "The work of God for you is to believe in the one whom he has sent to you." *That*, we say, is the crux of the faith! And since we do believe in Jesus, therefore we are doing good works. That is exactly what I thought —"Only believe," and spirituality is automatic.

But when I read the Sermon on the Mount, I was puzzled and uncomfortable; it seemed so full of impossible demands, so uncompromising—and so contradictory. "Let your light shine like that [the town on top of a hill, the lamp on a lamp-stand] in the sight of men," Jesus said. "Let them see the good things you do and praise your Father in Heaven." What good things? I wondered. He had been talking about humility, godly sorrow, a yearning for goodness, mercy, sincerity and peacemaking; even, most distressing of all, joy under persecution for the sake of the faith. Most of those things are attitudes, or qualities of soul. Is that what men are to see? Are those good works?

As I read further, however, I discovered that Jesus spoke sternly against doing good deeds conspicuously, advising his hearers to perform their charitable deeds so secretly that the left hand knew nothing of what the right hand was doing.

Shining Up My Good Works

How contradictory! To be told to let one's light shine, to let men see our good works which, presumably, they would attribute to God's presence in our lives—and then to be told to keep it all quiet lest we get no reward at all from God, only recognition from men. And how did this all square with Jesus' flat statement in John that the work of God was simply to believe in Him?

What *did* Jesus mean by good works—simply believing in him, developing certain attitudes, or doing "good" things? I leaned toward the first, and furthermore, was already deeply involved in shining up my "good works" of belief in Jesus Christ by immersing myself in books about prayer and the devotional life, in grimly determined Bible study and ill-timed and insensitive attempts to witness for Jesus.

It was in deep earnestness and with the utmost sincerity that I read all the books on prayer and witnessing. I was serious about my commitment to Christ, and I wanted to do everything the right way. After all, I had old habit patterns to rely on; it was like being in school. If one wanted to excel, one studied and concentrated and after awhile the subject was mastered. This was one more subject.

It seemed to follow logically that if the good works God wanted were belief in Jesus, then the more one knew the more one could believe, and the more one prayed the more faith one had, and the more one witnessed the more spiritual one was, and that, of course, meant more knowledge of him, hence—more good works. I didn't think it all out that coldly. But in a vague, shapeless way that's the conclusion I had come to. Belief in Jesus, properly attended to by all these spiritual exercises must lead to good works in the end.

I did not abandon that point of view overnight. It grew thin over the years and finally wore away entirely, battered and torn and shredded by the realities of life. One of those realities was the many people who believed in Jesus. They believed all the right things about him—how correct their doctrine, how unyielding their faith, how regular their spiritual exercises, how full of zeal they were!

I found them all very depressing. How dreadful it would be if they really knew me, knew what I was like inside the image I hid behind, got a glimpse of me when I was being myself. I knew I was, in spite of assiduous attention to all my spiritual exercises, still consumed with selfishness, hag-ridden by envy, occasionally overwhelmed by feelings of malice or unholy anger. How such people would condemn me!

And yet, these who believed with such rectitude were lacking in the kind of good works Jesus talked about in the Beatitudes. They were not merciful; they read people out of the fellowship right and left for all sorts of "sins," from the slightest deviation from *their* understanding of theology to the merest appearance of being worldly. Nor were they humble. They were delighted with their own spirituality and conveyed their satisfaction in every testimony meeting. As for claiming nothing (the meek), they expected everything, especially important positions in the church. It seemed to have evaded their attention that Jesus advised his followers to do their good deeds inconspicuously, since they were fond of relating what great blessings God had given them because (1) they tithed or gave even more generously to the church, (2) they witnessed with unflagging zeal and in general were examples of Christian rectitude.

Something else was going on in my life, however, which was stronger and bigger and more real than the guilt inflicted by my contrasting myself with these "successful" Christians. God was giving Russ and me friends, surrounding us and buttressing us with unpretentious Christians who were a source of help and pleasure. Both of us (though we certainly were not conscious of it at that time) were being made more like what God wanted us to be, not perfectly of course, but nevertheless changed into his pattern for us. This was being accomplished, not by a barrage of good advice, or testimonies, or pious examples, but by friends.

Gradually, but with a deepening conviction, we began to realize that the "good works" Jesus talked about were being offered up to us—had been offered up to us freely, unselfconsciously, for years, in the form of friendship. What really made the difference in our lives during times of stress was not some truth, a series of abstract propositions or moral principles. For a few people, perhaps, abstractions and principles may be important; but most of us are helped, or hurt, by other people. It may even be that abstract ideas have their greatest reality when they are embodied in people. I can believe in mercy as a concept and that God is merciful only because I've received mercy from people. Kindness would be just a word without content if I hadn't been treated kindly by someone. The only way God—who is to human beings the ultimate abstract—could get through to us and make himself real to us was in the form of a person, Jesus Christ. He still makes himself real through persons.

Our friends demonstrated to us that life is a whole—that we do not have one segment marked "spiritual," another "intellectual," another "emotional." They did this unintentionally, by being all of a piece; everything they did was part of their relationship to God, their spiritual life. Although we didn't use the word then, they were demonstrating that life is sacramental, that every action embodies in visible, tangible form a spiritual reality.

I began to learn then that what we are is of first importance. It is the source of what we do and what we say and what we think. My own efforts began to be less and less on polishing a set of good works in the "spiritual" area of my life and more on being—a good friend, a merciful person, a loving wife and mother.

Russ and I found ourselves carried gently along in the Christian life by our friends whose lives made what they said and what they did credible to us. They didn't think of themselves as "ministering" to us (a good work). Such pretentious thinking would have been laughed at. They didn't think at all about what their friendship was doing for us. That is the secret—and the glory—of the whole thing. Their friendship *was* a ministry without self-consciousness or silly pretensions.

There is a counterfeit friendship, of course. People do "take on" others with a kind of superficial friendship, in order to do them good—and sometimes the recipients are helped. God is gracious enough to use the poorest and most hypocritical efforts. But that kind of "project" friendship never does what a real, genuine, giving of oneself as a friend and receiving the other equally as a friend, can do. Friendship is always a two-way street. We give—and we receive. To be a friend simply in order to give is benevolence, not friendship. Genuine friendship needs no excuse for existing.

It was through the people who were and are our friends that God worked his own "good works" in our lives. And eventually I came to see that the good works he intended for us to do included both the attitudes of the Beatitudes and the actions of the Sermon on the Mount, as well as a host of delightful surprises I would never have dreamed of. Friends introduced us to new interests, new experiences, and new horizons.

III

WITHOUT
CONDITIONS

FRIENDSHIP is an intricate, complex affair which can never be defined and always has some element of mystery. Why do we "just naturally" like some people and find it easy to be with them, when others either leave us indifferent or even repel us? We can usually find reasons for not liking a certain person but cannot always pinpoint what it is that attracts us.

We might just as well leave it at that: friendship is a gift from God. We can cultivate it and see it grow and bloom, or let it die of neglect. But we can't "make" friendship. There must be an element of spontaneity or mutual recognition for a relationship to be called "friendship."

The Many Faces Of Friendship

Very early in our Christian lives, Russ and I found that some of our fellow church members assumed that being Christians automatically made us all friends; we ought to feel the same toward everyone. For awhile we tried to have that kind of friendship with everyone, but it just didn't work. I don't believe it was ever meant to work. After all, there are millions and millions of Christians in the world; and even if one felt obliged to be friends only with those in one's immediate locality, it would be impossible. There just isn't time to get acquainted, let alone be friends.

"Birds of a feather flock together" is an old saying which conveys the idea that people in groups have some identifying mark upon them, something that brings them together, or distinguishes them from others. It doesn't mean that the members of such a group are all identical (although that may be, in some cases), but simply that they share some common denominator.

That common bond, as far as Christians are concerned, is our mutual commitment to Christ. This one factor is of such enormous importance to us that it often weighs more than everything that might otherwise keep us apart. It doesn't cancel out differences in temperament and personality, however, although some Christians think it should. The Christian community is a unity which includes diversity.

It has always seemed to me that since God obviously likes diversity—he made his world such a delightful conglomeration of wildly different things and people—there must be plenty of room in the Christian family for all sorts of people. We're going to find, within the family group, some friends with whom we have special rapport, not just on the basis of our faith, but as total persons.

Natural affinities are part of God's plan for our lives. We

aren't just thrust into the Christian world willy-nilly, but we are put into a family—the Christian family. True, families don't always get along together, yet love is necessary if the harmony is to be preserved. Yes, *love* is *demanded* of us. Those who tried to be friends with everyone to exactly the same degree were confusing friendship with love.

About love, Jesus told us that God "makes his sun rise upon evil men as well as good, and he sends his rain upon honest and dishonest men alike. For if you love only those who love you, what credit is that to you? Even tax-collectors do that!" There are two clues in this statement to the nature of love—both God's love and human love.

God loves impartially both those who love him back and those who hate him or ignore him. He makes no distinction in the way the world runs between his special children and those who are the farthest from knowing or reverencing him. Jesus gave new content to the word "love." In the world, we love those who love us; but in God's family we begin to acquire the imprint of his love, so different from the best that this world knows that it is called by a different name: grace. Grace, the favor given to those who do not deserve it at all. That is God's love for us. Once we are his, we begin, however feebly and imperfectly to love others like that. Our best is never more than a whisper compared to the blazing reality of his grace; but however weak and faltering our love is, it is given us to use—it is demanded of us.

This love which the Bible pictures and God commands us to have for one another is a passionate concern for the good of the other person. It is something therefore that can be willed. That concern is expected of each one of us for every other member of the Christian family. But friendship is not demanded. We do not have to be friends with everyone, share their interests, enjoy their company—we must only will their good, that is, love them.

Like the rain that falls on the just and unjust alike, friendship is an undeserved gift of God—in a sense an extra. Taken up into the context of the Christian life it gains new dimensions, acquires depth and solidity and undreamed-of good. I think that friendship is one of God's secret means of working his will in the world. As such it is far less susceptible to corruption than many things God uses.

For one thing, there's less temptation to pride. After all, what virtue is there in simply accepting and enjoying a natural affinity for someone who (how delightful) happens also to be a Christian? It's not quite like taking on some task, such as serving as a Sunday school teacher, or being an officer in women's work, or even joining a class on how to be a better witness for Christ. One can always feel a satisfactory little glow of pride in these endeavors, rejoice in remembering that, after all, it's not everyone who is willing to take on these responsibilities.

But friendship? It's like being born with curly hair; one just thanks God for the delight of it, with none of the nonsense of self-congratulation. There is much more likely to be a sense of humility, of wonder that *they* should like and accept me. Sometimes this feeling is neurotic, born out of a low self-image, and tending to make one oversensitive and anxious to please. I rather think such anxieties about one's own worth are more common to human experience than a happy, unselfconscious expectation of being liked.

My own secret self-estimate is the anxious one. It is the frame of mind into which I fall when I am tired, or not well, or uneasy about something I've said or done. It is the habitual set of mind that was mine before I became a Christian. Although I know that God loves and accepts me and that my friends love and accept me, this old, unhealthy self-denigration still comes over me at times of physical or mental fatigue.

In talking with my friends, I've discovered we all have similar attitudes of self-doubt and unworthiness. There is healing for those wounds, however, and friendship is one of the remedies God uses. Friendship, like love, is never earned. It is either there—in embryonic form, at first—or not. One can do nothing to earn friendship, except just to be a friend.

I know that many of us, in our longing for friendship, do try to earn it by an inordinate attempt to please, by flattery, sometimes by toadying; but that is a sick sort of approach, born out of our inner uncertainties about our own worth as a friend. Unless one is really quite neurotic, the tendency to do this is something we're aware of and can guard against. And there is nothing quite so effective in squashing such a depressing estimate of oneself as the discovery that we *are* liked and found worthy of friendship *even when we're not* trying.

That was the repeated discovery Russ and I made.

We had grown up, as nearly everyone but a precious fortunate few grow up, finding that to be liked, one must be likable. This attitude is both natural and inevitable—and within limits very good. After all, to expect to be liked in spite of being disagreeable and thoughtless and careless of the feelings of everyone around is supremely egotistic.

But a desire to be accepted and liked can create an inner anxiety, especially in those who have been rebuffed in their attempts at friendship. Neurotic people are obsessed by fears of their own unworthiness, and go to extreme lengths to earn friendship. Though they are not alone in their anxiety, they just have more of it than most of us.

The Many Faces Of Friendship

When we first came into the Christian group which became, in a sense, our "family," Russ and I were just on the edge of becoming neurotic about our worthiness as friends. We had had some disappointing experiences, and we were wary. A revolutionary change in our lives came about because of the way we were received by some of the people we met. (It would have been too much to expect that everyone we met treated us kindly as friends.)

God used those with whom we had some natural affinities to bring us closer to him—through friendship. There were enough characteristics about us to nullify any common bonds we might have had with the Christians we got to know. We were overlaid with a veneer of almost sneering sophistication, which hid all our inward longings and hid them very well. We were not really attractive people, but we were welcomed as if we were.

No one talked to us about changing either our attitudes or our habits. Nothing was ever said that made us feel we were "projects." We got together for dinners and potlucks and picnics in the parks, and we talked about all the things young couples discuss: the men's jobs, their hobbies, our children, our problems with budgets, our hopes for the future. The only thing that was different—and it was the overwhelming, but hidden ingredient that made the friendship between us different from ordinary relationships—was the Christian commitment that underlay the thinking and conversation of everyone we were with.

Not that we sat around and discussed spiritual matters, or talked about our faith. When we did, at times, it was a natural outcome of our daily concerns and conversations. But whether we talked specifically about Christ or not, we were *in Christ* and our conversation was spiritual conversation because it was all a part of the grand whole that God was working out in our lives. God loves us as total people, not just as pawns who are only important when they are moved onto the square marked "church work," "Bible study," "prayer," or "talking about one's faith." Everything we do, think, say, is part of his total work in us, including our times together with other friends, whether or not we labeled our activities "spiritual."

None of us had any idea what potent forces were at work in our lives through such a simple, uncomplicated thing as friendship. We didn't even know we were changing our attitudes and goals in life, it was all happening so naturally and so gradually.

Now, looking back, I can see what was taking place. We were "catching" the Christian faith, simply by being with friends whose relationship to Christ was genuine. There was no artificial, trumped-up "witnessing," no little exhortations to shape up, or to change our way of living. But all the while we were changing—being changed.

As friendships were growing, we learned that natural affinities are not always immediately apparent. In fact some people who began by having a faint dislike for us (for our self-centered concern for money, perhaps, or for our veneer of hardness) ended up by becoming close friends. They put up with all they didn't like about us until they knew us well enough to see that the obvious and unacceptable traits were not all there was to us. We were not aware that we were receiving undeserved mercies, of course, because we didn't see ourselves as we really were—brittle, prickly, brash, and self-centered.

The fact that we were accepted just as we were was the single biggest factor in our lives at that time. We were finding it much easier to believe that Christ accepted us, because we were accepted by his people. The pattern of his life is lived out again and again in the lives of ordinary Christians, and where that is taking place, lives are being changed whether we see it or not.

There was a long, long way for us to go, of course. We were just beginning to discover what it is like to be part of the family of God. We had not yet learned that being accepted means we must also be accepting toward others. I am still learning that. But the new life had begun; we were on our way.

IV
WHAT
MONEY
CAN'T
BUY

FRIENDSHIP includes accepting each other in spite of attitudes or habits that are irritating, and even unChristian. The person who waits for someone to "shape up" before admitting him to his life is *not* a friend. Russ and I had some unpleasant attitudes when we became Christians, and these did not immediately dissolve. I suppose the first thing anyone would have observed about us was our obsessive desire for money.

To us, money meant status. Not that we didn't have a healthy desire for the good things money can buy—we did. But deeper than that, more powerful than that, more bruising to our self-esteem, was the knowledge that in this world most of us are judged and accepted or rejected on the basis of our financial standing.

That gnawing desire for money because it means one *is* someone, because it buys all the trappings of success, didn't vanish overnight when we began to take Christ seriously. It was far too deeply embedded in our thinking to be rooted out easily.

Both of us, having grown up during the deepest days of the depression, and having been without most of the material advantages of life, had an inner uneasiness about our place in the world. Although we deplored materialism, it was and is a major factor in the thinking of all of us in the Western world, even within the church. People are impressed by money and the things it buys, by the houses and cars and mode of living money makes possible; so much so that, without ever thinking it through, most of us just drift into the frame of mind that says, "So-and-so is a person worth knowing because he has money." Sometimes we spiritualize this attitude and justify it by saying that surely a man who has had the brains and the courage to make so much money must be a worthwhile person.

Russ and I had met that attitude many times in church groups, as well as its corollary: that if one doesn't have more than an average income, if there is always the necessity to weigh alternatives when spending because there isn't enough to buy everything one wants, one has the uneasy, lurking conviction that one is at fault as a person. Oh, there are exceptions. Clergymen are not expected to be wealthy, but we often regard them as a set-apart group of people, called by God to do without the things money can buy in order to accomplish a special task. *That* is certainly no New Testament concept; rather it calls every Christian to work hard at whatever he is doing, and the same obligations and responsibilities are laid upon everyone.

Natural affinities have a great deal to do with making friends. But money is not a natural affinity; it is something one has acquired. When money becomes a factor in choosing—or rejecting—possible friends, it kills any chance of a genuine relationship. Of course, we must realistically face the fact that there are often such vast differences between the way people with large incomes and those with more modest salaries live that the differences can be an impossible barrier to friendship. But this is not an infallible rule. I know people in various parts of the country whose circle of friends encompasses a wide scope financially, from professors on the unexceptional salary that small colleges usually pay, to business and professional men in very high income tax brackets.

Where such friendships do occur, the important fact to remember is that the common bond they share, their Christian faith, also includes natural affinities which are not related to how much money anyone has. Good friendships are possible only where money *isn't* the most important factor in life, where it isn't used as a standard by which to measure others. Only when both the people with money and the people without money are mature enough to stop being self-conscious about their place in the world can they become friends.

Russ and I didn't know all this when we became Christians. We had all the awkward defensiveness that comes of doing without and hating it, that feels deeply the indifferent scorn of those on a higher financial level, and that has gotten some deep wounds along the way.

We were an odd combination of prickly sensitivity and brittle hardness. There was a wall around us, built up over the years so we wouldn't be hurt too much any more. With one part of our minds we decried materialism, we had harsh things to say about the falseness of judging everyone by what he had gathered to himself materially—and yet we were in bondage to the fear of that same judgment.

Sermons preached on the values of the kingdom of Heaven may have confirmed our inner conviction that money is not, indeed, the true measure of a man's worth. Bible lessons on the same subject, showing in detail what the teaching of the Bible is, were very helpful. But neither sermons nor Bible lessons have the force that human lives do; *that's* where friendship did the work that nothing and no one else—not even the minister, the teacher or the leader—can do. Friendship made the teaching of Jesus and the apostles believable.

Yet learning the true value of men and money was a laborious process for us. No church is made up of perfect people, only of people who know they need Christ, and are on the way. Our church was no exception. Some of the church people thought just as everyone else thinks about money. A goodly number, for various reasons, had never "gotten the message"; they were part of the church but had no idea of what the gospel was really all about. Therefore, even in the church, we were sometimes slapped in the face by totally materialistic standards. We expected established Christians to have better attitudes than we had. *We* were just beginning but we were willing to change.

We were not being realistic about the church, however. It isn't perfect and never has been. We found that James had covered the problem in his letter to one of the very first churches. He warned them in no uncertain words not to "combine snobbery with faith in our glorious Lord Jesus Christ!" If they gave preferential treatment to a well-dressed man and snubbed a shabbily dressed, obviously poor man "you are making class distinctions in your mind, and setting your-selves up to assess a man's quality," he told them, "a very bad thing. . . . Once you allow any invidious distinctions to creep in," he added, "you are sinning; you have broken God's Law."

In the centuries of the church's history, the command to allow no distinctions in the church because of status or money has been disobeyed, disobeyed in all branches of the church, in all communions. And yet, in spite of all one can say about what's wrong, and has always been wrong, with the church, there is another side to the story. Quietly, usually unnoticed and unremarked, the church has been carried on its way by ordinary men and women, some richer than others, who were free of the slavery to money that excessive devotion brings —men and women who just went about their business being Christians, and being friends.

That was the happy experience Russ and I found eventually. In spite of our defensiveness, in spite of our anxiety, and also in spite of our veneer of sophistication and self-confidence, we were met by friendship which disarmed us and began to break down that wall we had built.

Several young couples in Homebuilders Class used to get together and have potluck dinners. None of us could have afforded at that time to put on a dinner party. Few of us had the china, or silver, or crystal that every young couple assumes will be theirs when they marry these days. World War II had not been over long, and we were all trying to reestablish ourselves in jobs. We were thinking about buying homes—tract homes, of course, on a low down-payment. Fur-niture was usually a hodgepodge of hand-me-downs and bar-gain basement pieces. No, we didn't have a lot of this world's goods, but we did have friends, and we were beginning to discover that it really doesn't make much difference whether you eat steak or meat loaf if you're having a good time with compatible people.

We were learning that financial success does not seem to be a New Testament concept. On the contrary, God's people met all kinds of trials with almost monotonous regularity. They were misunderstood, persecuted even to physical punishment and the most cruel deaths men can devise; they often lived precarious lives. Nowhere does one read anything remotely suggesting that the Christian life brings prosperity.

Prosperity comes because of hard work, fortuitous circumstances, a talent for making money—none of which are either Christian or non-Christian. Sometimes wealth is the result of less than honest manipulations, or of outright crookedness. Having money says nothing about one's spiritual state and indicates nothing about the worth of a person. That idea is part of the secular world's thinking. Christians are never immune, however, from adopting the thinking of the non-Christian world around us; either we are so blind or the forms of thought so subtle that we fail to recognize them. C. S. Lewis remarked in *Screwtape Letters* that of the three great standard temptations—the World, the Flesh, and the Devil—the World was sadly underestimated as a deadly danger.

An idolatrous attitude toward money is only one aspect of secular thinking, but it is certainly one of the most prevalent marks of the godless man, simply because it is *the* symbol of power. It is not too surprising, therefore, when this almost religious reverence toward money can be found in the church. Jesus was talking to religious men when he warned, "No one can be loyal to two masters. He is bound to hate one and love the other, or support one and despise the other. You

cannot serve God and the power of money at the same time."
He knew how fatally easy it would always be for his people
to slip back into the old, comfortable way of evaluating a
man's worth—by what he possesses.

Because of the insidiousness of this temptation, the wonder
is that there are so many Christians who, whether they have
money or not, have come to see it as quite irrelevant to a
man's real value. It was a long time before Russ and I discovered that some of the friends we had come to know very
well were financially far better off than most of us. They were
so unostentatious in their manner of living, so free from any
desire to impress anyone by a great display of possessions that
most of us were unaware of their prosperity. When we did
begin to become aware that certain of our friends had a lot
of money, and yet were not unduly impressed by it, we began
to be free ourselves.

Our bondage, you see, was just as terrible as that of a miser.
It doesn't matter whether one has money or not, if he thinks
about it all the time he's a slave to it. The shackles were
loosened when we began to see that among Christian friends
money is not a determining factor in a relationship.

It can be told so simply, and yet it took so long for us to
learn! And, because we usually went overboard on everything
we learned, for a time we were just as obnoxious in our determination *not* to be judged by our financial standing as we
had been in our anxiety to succeed so we'd have the status
money brings. The pendulum swings, of course, and eventually
we became less intense about the subject of money, so that
we could accept new friends who had money as easily as those
on our own level. And *that* is just as difficult as giving up
the idea that money makes a man worthwhile.

V

THE

GENUINE

ARTICLE

I DO NOT remember that anyone "witnessed" to Russ and me in the popular sense of the word; that is, talked to us about what Christ had done for him or treated us to a little spiritual homily. It may have happened, of course, but if we were the recipients of that kind of witness, it made little or no impression. What I do remember, vividly, is that we were getting to know people whose lives attracted us and whose friendship we valued.

And yet I look back and see that we were being witnessed to in the best New Testament tradition. These people were really serving us—looking after our need for friends and for understanding—and doing it all because they were our friends, they cared about us.

I see the pattern for such service in Jesus' own life. Whenever people would listen to him, he talked to them about God, about the kingdom of God and what they needed to do to get into it. He healed sick people when he met them, and he had compassion on the poor outcasts of the social structure of the day with whom he spent time—he was their friend. The writers of the Gospels particularly noticed his sympathy for people, and repeatedly described how Jesus "had compassion on them"—the sick, the maimed, the aimless. He had compassion. He had concern, pity, sympathy, whatever word you want to call it. And he acted on his compassion.

Sometimes we are told that he followed an act of healing by some spiritual instruction; other times, we are told simply that he healed the crowds who came to him. Whatever he did, he acted because he really cared about all the people he met. He cared most of all, I'm sure, about their ultimate destiny—their relationship to God—but he never made the fatal mistake of dividing them up into separate compartments and ignoring one part of their lives while trying to do something good for the other part. He always saw the total person, loved the total person, helped the total person.

The night before his death, Jesus washed his disciples' feet, an act which shocked and horrified them because it was the sort of menial service the very lowest of servants did. Dirty, smelly feet to be washed and dried, feet that had been out all day in the hot middle-eastern dusty roads—that was for slaves, that kind of service. Jesus, however, insisted on performing the task; then he said—possibly with some sternness—"Do you realize what I have just done to you? You call me 'teacher' and 'Lord' and you are quite right, for I am your teacher and your Lord. But if I, your teacher and Lord, have washed your feet, you must be ready to wash one another's feet. I have given you this as an example so that you may do as I have done. Believe me, the servant is not greater than his master and the messenger is not greater than the man who sent him. Once you have realized these things, you will find your happiness in doing them."

In that way he acted out a parable for them. They were his friends, and he had served them as a slave serves a master. At the same time *he* was their Lord and master. If they were to be really his friends, they must be ready to serve each other as he had served them. Later he said, "There is no greater love than this—that a man should lay down his life for his friends. You are my friends if you do what I tell you to do. I shall not call you servants any longer, for a servant does not share his master's confidence. No, I call you friends, now, because I have told you everything that I have heard from the Father."

They were his friends—he had confided in them, told them all that he had received from the Father. They were his friends and he had served them. Now he commanded them to serve each other in the same way, doing the most despised tasks. It all seems so clear, doesn't it? Not necessarily attractive at first glance, because it runs contrary to everything we naturally believe in, and contrary to all our patterns of thinking which are part and parcel of the world around us.

Perhaps that is why we are so reluctant to take it seriously. In the Middle Ages, kings and noblemen acted out this parable, washing the feet of the poor on Maundy Thursday. But they did it only once a year, and it was a symbol of service that few of them ever carried further than that one ceremony. We, however, are commanded to take all this quite seriously;

in fact, we are called to live like that consistently—as friends, but as friends who serve each other.

The service we give each other is often so unconspicuous that it goes unnoticed by most people. It doesn't mean ostentatious "good deeds," meant to be seen by everyone and commented on. It may mean many different things in many different situations; but it will always signify Jesus' love being taken seriously.

After Russ and I became involved in our church and in smaller groups, we found ourselves being served in this Christian graciousness. Most of the time, however, we weren't aware of a relationship of service. What we *were* aware of was a quality of life which attracted us as nothing else had ever done, a quality of friendship that met our deepest needs. We knew we had never found such friends outside the Christian world. Beyond that, I can't remember analyzing it too much, or ever thinking of their friendship in terms of service. But that is just what it was.

For instance someone would call and offer to pick us up on the way to a Bible study group, or some other gathering. A group getting together for a spur-of-the-moment potluck would include us because they knew we were lonely. In a thousand nameless ways we were served by those who had become our friends in the truly Christian sense of the word. They were serving us, not with ostentatious good deeds meant to be remarked upon by others, but by being available, being in tune with our needs, and sometimes by being greatly inconvenienced for our sakes.

They were not doing all this as a subtle means of witnessing to us, although that is exactly what the result was. They *were* what Christ wanted them to be, and so they were his witnesses to us of the kind of life he intends his people to have. Because they did what was obviously needed, and we accepted it in that same spirit—the spirit of friendship—something good was accomplished among us.

The other way of witnessing—where one does something not because there is a need, but because it will be a "witness" often fails in its purpose. One of the principles Jesus emphasized is that things must be what they seem to be; no pretence, no hypocrisy. Jesus made some rather severe judgments on those whose actions are not what they seem: "Beware of doing your good deeds conspicuously *to catch men's eyes* or you will miss the reward of your Heavenly Father. . . .when you pray, don't be like the playactors. They love to stand and pray in the synagogues and at street corners so that people may see them at it. Believe me, they have had all the reward they are going to get!"

Paul made truth practical. He talked about brotherly love, about honesty in all one's dealings, about forbearance and tolerance for one another's weaknesses, about sexual purity. He instructed parents in their relationships toward each other and toward their children, advised children to obey their parents, had something to say in several letters about both employers and employees. In short, he talked about how one lives the ordinary, everyday life most men live.

Paul's mention of preaching is usually a reference to his own or another apostle's activities. He wrote in his letter to the Ephesians, "Some he [God] made his messengers, some prophets, some preachers of the gospel." He often refers to the effect all Christians have on the world around them. "We Christians have the unmistakable 'scent' of Christ," he told the Corinthians, "discernible alike to those who are being saved and to those who are heading for death. To the latter if seems like the deathly smell of doom; to the former it has the refreshing fragrance of life itself." To the Philippians, he advised, "Do all you have to do without grumbling or arguing, so that you may be God's children, blameless, sincere and wholesome, living in a warped and diseased world, and shining there like lights in a dark place. For you hold in your hands the very word of life."

Those words are an accurate description of many Christians I know. Some are teachers, devoting endless hours to helping their pupils become mature adults as well as educated ones. The women who work in offices where complaining, slacking on work and undercutting each other are the accepted way of behaving stand out because they don't do these things. It may not be showy to "do all you have to do without grumbling or arguing," but it is certainly noticed—and remembered—by those around. This kind of living may not be our conception of witnessing, but it fits the New Testament picture.

The apostles were constantly reminding their fledgling Christians that some were called to preach, teach, or do other specifically marked-off activities, but that *all* men were called to be witnesses. To *be* witnesses—by their lives. There are only *two* specific references to what we would call witnessing—talking to non-Christians about Christ—in the New Testament letters. One occurs toward the end of Paul's letter to the church at Colossae. "Be wise in your behavior towards non-Christians," he wrote them, "and make the best possible use of your time. Speak pleasantly to them, but never sentimentally, and learn how to give a proper answer to every questioner."

Paul must have assumed that the quality of life shown by the Christians would elicit some queries from the pagans in Colossae. *What makes you so kind and loving? What makes you have the attitude of forgiveness toward those who trample*

*all over you and wrong you? Why don't you stand up for
your rights? Why don't you take advantage of these situations
to make yourself a little extra cash?* We can imagine how such
questions would come, in all sorts of situations. Paul told the
Christians to be ready with a proper answer, to be pleasant
and to give a clear reason for their way of living—that is,
to have a genuine testimony.

Earlier Paul had written to the Thessalonian Christians that
their lives were so utterly different after their commitment
to Christ that they were being talked of all through Macedonia
and Achaia, as well as other places. How they lived caused
the comment, and while they no doubt were ready enough
to tell those who asked them what had happened to change
their lives, it was the new kind of living itself that made the
difference.

The other reference to what we like to call "witnessing"
is found in Peter's first letter: "Your conduct among the
surrounding peoples in your different countries should always
be good and right, so that although they may in the usual
way slander you as evildoers, yet when disasters come they
may glorify God when they see how well you conduct your-
selves." That's not exactly a cheery little word. It implies that
Christians will be slandered—and they certainly were during
those early centuries. It also implies that their conduct during
times of disaster will be the witness God uses in the world.
Most of us today would rather talk about what Christ has
done for us in making life better, solving our problems, reliev-
ing our burdens, or smoothing out some difficulty, and skip
the disasters.

So much has been said by Christians about how God has
solved their financial problems, healed their illnesses, straight-
ened out their erring children—or wives—or husbands—that

we seem to be preaching a Christ entirely different from the New Testament Christ. He did not call his disciples to an easy life. He did not promise to take away all their difficulties. Quite the opposite. He warned them to count the cost of discipleship, told them they'd have trouble in the world, and never promised them worldly ease or success.

Here, then, are two kinds of witnessing. The New Testament kind of witness consists of a life which is, in its quality of adherence to Jesus' principles and person, so unusual that it brings forth questions. The other is a kind of semi-professional preaching, when we feel we must talk to people and convince them of the claims of Christ. This kind of witnessing often does bring results. We must be very careful not to criticize anyone who is striving to do God's work in the world. But it does contain a built-in danger, a tendency that may result in a sort of super-sell approach: Christ is presented much like some modern deodorant or mouthwash—something to make life better, to get what one wants out of life. And that is a far cry from the Christ of the New Testament.

Friendship, honestly and wholeheartedly given, is the first kind of witnessing. It is something all of us can do, because we all can be friends. It is free of the dangers the second kind of witnessing carries with it, particularly the tendency to pride. At the same time it does cost something. It means being "out in the world," making friends with people. It means getting involved in their lives, helping them with their difficulties, being good neighbors—as the good Samaritan was. He must have been considerably inconvenienced by having to interrupt his business trip carting a wounded stranger to an inn and taking care of him, not to mention leaving money with the landlord. We are never told whether he got it back. That is the kind of friendship Russ and I were won by.

There were many times along the way when, but for that kind of friendship, we would have given up the whole Christian business. No doubt some tiny residue of faith would have remained, but we would have been stunted, undeveloped Christians the rest of our lives, as many people have become on leaving the church.

My own father, who died early this year, was just such a man. I have never known anyone whose integrity and honesty were greater than his, but at times he lacked tolerance toward the weaknesses of others and was inclined to be harsh in his judgments. He needed the balance of Christian friends, but he remained very distant from the church for all the years my brothers and I were growing up, and he said plenty about the reasons for his attitude.

As a young man, he had been full of enthusiasm for Christian work, and was always active in young people's work. Time after time after time he was disillusioned and hurt by the leaders—and sometimes the ministers themselves—whose shabby lives made lies of their testimony. One minister even approached my father once and asked him to intercede with a civic board for an elder of his church, though he admitted there were good reasons why the man did not deserve a position on the board. My father used to speak with the utmost love and respect of a minister he had known as a young man, a Dr. Kingsbury. That one man was the only balance in favor of the good Christian life—the scales were so weighted on the other side by men whose lives made nonsense of their public testimony.

That's no excuse, of course, for my father's remaining critical of the church. Yet he is only one example of many hundreds who stay out of the churches because they are turned off by Christians as they see them operate in daily life.

The Many Faces Of Friendship

If dishonesty in business is a scandal that hampers the work of the church, so is dishonesty in personal relationships. We cheat those to whom we offer a pretend friendship without the reality behind it, even though we do it in the name of Christ. To go through the motions of friendship in order to get the opportunity to give a Christian witness wrongs both parties to the relationship. The one offered such false coin is cheated, because there is no substance to the association, it's all a fake. The one professing a friendship that is merely a front, a gimmick to get a hearing for his case, cheats himself of any possible genuine relationship, because he has blocked it out with an illusion. He never really "sees" the person he has taken on as a project, he simply sees an object to be manipulated.

Over the years I've observed some sad instances of dishonesty. Sometimes Christians have been unethical and wrong in their business dealing. I've seen dishonesty in personal relationships, a counterfeit friendship used as a vehicle for witnessing. Such hypocrisy is discouraging. But it is not the whole story of the church. Outnumbering the crippled Christians who can't be straight in business, or the deluded Christians who can't be real in a relationship because they are using it as a front for their spiritual "thing," are the countless everyday, ordinary Christians who go about just being themselves. They work, play, make friends, all with transparent simplicity. They *are* the "genuine article."

These were the kind of people who kept Russ and me in the church when the going was rough. These were the people who made the difference when we were tempted to give it all up. They are everywhere today—not showy or shiny with a professional Christian polish, but quietly doing the work of the kingdom just by *being* themselves.

VI
BEING
WHAT
WE
ARE

IS PERSONAL honesty possible? I mean honesty in our relationships with each other—not just the honesty that prevents our assuming a façade of friendship in order to witness, but an utter absence of "front" in all relationships. Is it possible to be completely what we are?

How can you tell the absolute truth at all times without being sometimes cruel, sometimes interfering, sometimes malicious, often wounding—and not helpful at all? "Little white lies" are what we call the social fibs we all use in order to smooth over, or avoid an awkward situation. We have all been in many situations in which the truth would have certainly hurt someone deeply. What are we to do in such circumstances?

We have the demands of Christ and the entire New Testament for honesty. Jesus told some of the Jews who were boasting about their descent from Abraham, and hence from God: "Your father is the devil, and what you are wanting to do is what your father longs to do. He always was a murderer, and has never dealt with the truth, since the truth will have nothing to do with him. Whenever he tells a lie, he speaks in character, for he is a liar and the father of lies."

None of us can claim to be always and completely truthful. As a matter of fact, the only entirely truthful person I have ever known was also the most disagreeable and unloving person I have ever known. And that is what complicates the situation—the fact that quite unpleasant people, who *like* saying malicious things and broadcasting the one fact someone most desires kept quiet, are so fond of calling themselves "honest."

"So the word of God became a human being and lived among us. We saw his splendor (the splendor as of a father's only son), full of grace and truth." Dr. Richard Langford once said, in discussing this verse, that Jesus Christ was the only human being who was a perfect blend of grace and truth. All of us are sadly overbalanced one way or another. If we have grace, we are not as truthful as we might be; it is so much easier to make things pleasant for everyone than to deal in harsh realities. If we are truthful, we are lacking in grace—*never mind people's feelings, say what is so, describe conditions as they are, and let the chips fall where they may.*

In order to come anywhere near the balance Christ had, we must admit that none of us will ever be perfectly honest *and* perfectly full of grace at the same time. We are human, and to be human means to be fallible. None of us will ever be able to communicate perfectly with anyone else; being human, among other things, means being "unfinished," so to speak. We all know what it means to want desperately to express ourselves—our emotions, convictions, *ourselves*—and be frustrated. We can't find words, there are no words, with which we can make ourselves transparent, even to those we love the most deeply.

So we start with a determination to be as honest as possible. Paul put it succinctly: "Finish, then, with lying and tell your neighbor the truth. For we are not separate units but intimately related to each other in Christ."

Honesty, being what we seem to be, is necessary because we are not the separate little units we think we are, but are related parts of a whole. We belong to each other, because we belong to Christ. Our relationship to each other is in and through Christ, and although it is a spiritual relationship, it is nonetheless real. The responsibilities and privileges it carries with it are real.

Some superficial thinkers tend to dismiss the reality of the spiritual bond between members of the Christian family as being a symbolic thing. But symbols stand for a reality, or they wouldn't exist at all; the reality behind the symbols is too much for us to comprehend in our present state, but it is there. Our relationship to all Christians is a real one. We are *commanded*—not advised—to live honestly and harmoniously with each other because of it.

Living harmoniously, however, is not a simple matter of just telling the truth at all times—"speaking plainly," as one friend put it once. It is a matter of our total selves in relationship with others. One can say a thing which is entirely true—as far as the facts go—and be dishonest in intent and purpose, and in the effect produced.

The honest friendship which was so attractive to Russ and me was a friendship offered without subterfuge or ulterior motives. It was based on the fact that Christ loved us all, and we all belonged to him—plus that certain indefinable something I have called, for lack of a better definition, natural affinity. The honesty we were all learning to develop in our lives as Christians was an honesty of intent and purpose, not merely of speech.

There were times when complete candor on the part of some of our friends would have been less than honest because it would have destroyed the friendship between us. We weren't ready to accept some of the truths of life. Our friends' honest intent to be the best friends to us they could possibly be gave them the wisdom and the sensitivity to refrain from saying some things which, although true in themselves, would have been too much for us to take.

As we grew close, it was possible to be more open. I didn't realize, for instance, how obsessed I was with money (our lack of it) until a friend said in the middle of a discussion, "I wonder, Eileen, if you realize how much of your conversation is about money?" To write the words makes the sentence sound hard, but it wasn't. It could only have been said when our friendship had come to the place where I knew my friend loved me. I was caught up short, and in an instant realized how true the statement was. The constant, frustrating anxieties about lack of money, the multiplying wants in my life, were imprisoning me as surely as if I had been a miser obsessed with a secret hoard of gold. That was one of the great, liberating moments of my life. Not that the freedom from obsession with money and material wants just happened immediately.

Being What We Are

But I recognized the situation, knew its awful truth and its dangers, and determined to cope with it.

Most of the great breakthroughs in my Christian life have not come to me through the medium of a sermon or a Sunday school lesson, although I am sure both are part of the process. But the final, illuminating recognition of a new truth has nearly always come through something said by a dear friend. Many times, in talking later of what has happened, I've discovered to my amazement that the friend didn't even remember the conversation!

Russ and I were impatient people. We wanted to do so much, we wanted to achieve so much, and, as I said, we entered the Christian life encumbered by an obsessive desire for material success and all it brings. We did a lot of moving around, buying and selling of houses, in an effort to make money and better ourselves. Sometimes we acted impulsively and got ourselves in real financial difficulties.

After one of those foolish moves, we went to our friend and pastor, Dr. Richard C. Halverson, who was then one of the ministerial staff at the First Presbyterian Church of Hollywood. He taught the home Bible class we attended and was a trusted friend as well as our counselor. In his office we poured out our tale of woe.

When we had finished, he looked at us and sighed. "Russ and Eileen," he said finally, "whenever I look at you I see, written in letters of fire above your heads, the word W A I T."

Neither of us ever forgot those words. Afterwards, we could laugh about it, as we reminisced about old times. But then it was a cataclysmic revelation to us. It changed our lives, our entire attitude toward life.

The words could have been said in a sermon, addressed

generally to the congregation. Perhaps they were. I'm sure we've heard many sermons on patience, or on waiting on the Lord. But we weren't patient—and we needed to be told, face to face, by a friend, that that was hurting us. The truth had to be spoken directly to us, and it had to be spoken by a friend, in honesty, and wrapped in love. That's the only way we could have accepted it.

It's not true that when a relationship is good and clear, either in a family or between friends, one can say anything. The closer the relationship, the more need for sensitivity and tender regard for each other's feelings. Which hurts more—hard words from a stranger or casual acquaintance, or hard words from someone we love? Friendship is one of the most demanding and yet rewarding kinds of love, and it cannot thrive without an awareness of one another's needs, of the places where one treads softly if at all, and of the times when it's best to speak to the point.

The Apostle Paul was aware of this problem of human relations. "Finish then, with lying," he told the Ephesians, "and tell your neighbor the truth. For we are not separate units but intimately related to each other in Christ." This is very true. But his next sentence nails the truth to human situations and becomes intensely practical: "If you are angry, be sure that it is not out of wounded pride or bad temper. Never go to bed angry—don't give the devil that sort of foothold."

Now I have more than my share of pride, and so in the course of time I have sustained a great many wounds; that is inevitable, and it's been a good thing. Pride, unpricked and undeflated is always destructive in the end. Some years ago, at a Bible class we attended, my feelings were hurt. They were hurt because I was proud, and didn't take kindly to having my opinions shown up for nonsense. I'm ashamed now when I remember my infantile reaction of resentment and how I nursed my wounded feelings until they were ridiculously inflated.

I called Dick Halverson—who must have had the patience of an early martyr—and aired my grievance. There was a long silence. At last he said gently, "Eileen, why don't you let these occasions become a means of grace in your life?" I was brought up short. Why didn't I? What was grace for, if not for times when I would naturally respond with anger, or unkind words, or hurt feelings? The more I thought about it, the more logical—in the light of God's grace toward us—the idea seemed to be.

I'd like to say that since that day I have always unswervingly responded to situations that have tried my patience or hurt my feelings with the grace that comes from God. But it wouldn't be true; I haven't. That *has* been my goal, though, to live with something of God's grace in my life.

There is a counterfeit form of true friendship which is self-seeking, arrogant and without kindness. I have been deeply hurt by some I thought were friends. So has everyone. At such times I was helped by remembering Dick's advice to let the wound help me turn to God for his grace. Then I recall my own failures to be all a friend ought to be, just a *few* of the many times when my words or actions have undoubtedly wounded someone. I have been wounded by my friends because they aren't yet perfect, and they have been hurt by me. We need the grace of God not just when false friends make us unhappy but because all of us in our friendships occasionally fail. Who am I, to expect to get through life without ever being misunderstood or hurt or slighted? I cannot expect to be protected.

If Dick had responded with sympathy, or with an attempt to reason me out of my angry mood when I told him about my hurt feelings, nothing permanently good would have happened. True, he might have helped me avert making an immediate mistake which I would have later regretted; but that would have been the end of it. Honesty, given with the utmost love, was what was needed.

Since we are all, to some extent, defensive and protective, each of us with our various ways of warding off possible hurt, it will never be possible to have a totally open relationship with everyone. Some of us just can't take it. The honesty God wants us to show in our lives must be tempered by love, as well as by sensitivity and wisdom.

The friendships that endure through years seem to me to have a certain characteristic way of developing. First, one meets a new friend, or a new couple, and there is a mutual attraction. The friendship begins tentatively, exploring personalities, growing to know each other gradually. All is enthusiasm, on both sides. After a time, however, all the nice things are taken for granted, and the friendship has gotten to the point where each one begins to learn things about the other one which are irritating—or not at all admirable, or desirable. A season of disenchantment sets in when the rough edges of each personality grate on each other.

This is the crucial point in every friendship—perhaps even in every love affair. Here, it can all end. There may not be enough on the credit side to make it worth while carrying the relationship further. But if both or all of the persons concerned weather this period, then comes a genuine, bedrock friendship based on reality. Both the delightful things and the things one doesn't like so much are known and accepted by the people involved. They have at last built something worthy of the name "friendship." Anything less than this is mere acquaintance, or casual and rather superficial sociability.

It's hard, weathering the rough part of a developing relationship, but it's the only way any solid friendship is ever built. Honesty is part of it.

VII
FRIENDS
FOR
ALL
TIMES

NONE OF US like to think we are "average." We'd much rather think we are unique, so special that even our problems are different than other people's problems. However, honesty compels me to admit that our family, as the children were growing up, was a pretty average family.

In 1948 Russ and I were going through the usual struggles of a ten-year-old marriage. Russ was trying to get ahead in business. I was occupied with making too little money go farther than it was ever intended to, with P.T.A., church, frantic house cleaning, three children (eight, six, three and a half) in and out, and a dog. I was always a little bit under it. The frustrations of my never-ending wants (nicer furniture, better clothes, more money to entertain . . . and on and on), plus the fatigue of trying to keep what we had as nice looking as possible, made me cross-grained and irritable at times. In all of this, our new life was growing, but it was still a tender plant.

That summer we decided, in spite of our slender budget, to go to a family conference at Forest Home Christian Conference Center. Some of our friends were going for the week; others in the church whom we knew, although not so well, would be there. The speakers were highly recommended, and care for the children was offered. In addition to all this, it was quite inexpensive. We packed up the children and went.

Two or three days after the conference began, six-year-old Carole Ann was a little feverish and had symptoms of tonsilitis—a trouble she'd had before. There were two doctors also attending the conference, and they agreed there didn't seem to be too much wrong with her, but I kept her in our cabin. The next day three-year-old Donna developed a slight limp in her right leg, but she didn't complain too much, and with children that age there are always reasons for a limp. Indeed, Donna usually had a scab on one knee, which led me to believe she had taken another spill.

The next morning, however, as Carole Ann got out of bed and knelt down to get her shoes, she was simply unable to get up again. I called one of the doctors, and although he was puzzled about her symptoms, we all agreed that we ought to go home and get the girls to a doctor. None of us were aware of it, but Carole Ann and Donna were, that July, two of the many cases of polio that were to make the summer a horror.

By the time we had driven home, arranged for Darrell to

be taken care of, and gotten the girls to the General Hospital as the doctor had advised us, it was apparent that there was a strong possibility they did, indeed, have poliomyelitis. Neither of them had typical symptoms. They did not have the muscle spasms, nor any of the usual telltale signs of that frightening disease, but spinal taps showed something seriously amiss with the central nervous system of both children, and the diagnosis was made.

The rest of the summer was a nightmare. We drove back and forth to General Hospital, not being allowed to see them but unable to stay away. We watched Darrell anxiously, frightened if he so much as sneezed. And we began to get phone calls of all sorts.

Most of the calls were from friends and acquaintances in the church who were honestly concerned about Carole Ann and Donna, and who wanted to convey their sympathy and tell us they were praying for us. We had offers of financial help if we needed it, and many, many heartening expressions of love and encouragement. There were other calls, however, of a different nature.

Isn't it remarkable how eager people are to convey bad news? We were informed that (1) the entire family conference was in a great uproar over what had happened and the possibility that all the children had been exposed; (2) that many people were furious with us for not realizing that our children had something communicable and leaving the camp sooner, and (3) that So-and-so and his wife were frantic and were in a state of near collapse because their children might get polio, and so were many others. And on and on and on.

The two doctors, who had not realized any more than we did that we were part of a nationwide epidemic of poliomyelitis, were blamed in varying degrees. The phone rang and rang. Russ, of course, was working as usual. In those frantic days early in the epidemic, most unusual and rather hit-and-miss precautions were taken to halt its spread. Suspected persons were quarantined—no one was to come to our house—but the men were allowed to go to and from work as usual.

The worst thing of all was that some of the children most likely to have been exposed by Carole Ann and Donna were the children of our closest friends. *They* were the ones, however, who were our stalwart supporters, who never by word or look reproached us or suggested we were to blame. They gave us heart to keep going, and literally kept our faith from disappearing.

We did feel guilty—who could have helped it in our position? We did regret, bitterly, our lack of foresight in not leaving the conference at once when Carole Ann became ill. The fact that at every conference, every year, some children and some adults got colds, and sometimes the flu, and nothing more, did not alter the fact that *this* time it had been far more serious and we were being held responsible.

One expects to be blamed at such a time, by almost everyone. But the bitterness of the feeling against us (which may have been exaggerated by our eager informants) shocked us. Did Christians behave this way too? Was there no place of refuge and acceptance, no company of people to whom we could turn in our trouble? Indeed, some of our neighbors, whose children had undoubtedly been exposed by ours before we left for the conference and who were not professing Christians at all, behaved with so much more forbearance than some of our fellow believers that the contrast was painfully sharp. We were distraught, and began to wonder if there was anything in a faith that seemed to do so little for most of its adherents.

Again, as in the first days of our experience as Christians, we were on the edge of giving the whole thing up—except for our friends. They were the deciding factor in our lives at that time, the only reason we held on to what feeble faith we had. We had the constant reassurance of Bob and Molly Ringer, whose boy Jerry, about Darrell's age, had been with our children constantly, as well as Marilyn and Loren Davies, whose son had also been close to our children. Bill and Mary Durning were another couple who gave us strong support, and there were others as well who surrounded us with love and help. They saved the day.

One momentous night, after a phone call from one of the men who had been at the conference told me the bad news about all the people who were angry with us, we sat down and talked the whole matter out. While I had been talking on the phone, Russ had been shouting at me to hang up. It's a good thing I had answered, rather than Russ, for the anxiety was beginning to tell on him and he would have met hard words with equally bitter ones. Not that I was such a tower of strength—I was simply doing what most women always do, trying to smooth things down and keep the situation under control.

Nevertheless, my feelings were lacerated, and so we talked for hours. Why had God let this catastrophe come upon us, just as we were trying, earnestly, to live the way he wanted us to? Why, when we already had so many hard places in life to cope with, were we given another? The outcome as far as Carole Ann and Donna were concerned was still in doubt. They did not seem to be in grave danger, although one of the doctors at General Hospital murmured ominously about some evidence of the dreaded bulbar polio in Carole Ann. There might well be severe crippling, however, and

65

there would certainly be a long time of treatment ahead. What were we to think?

In the end, we simply decided to hang on; just to hang on. We didn't get any answers to our questions, but where else could we go for help and strength for living if the Christian gospel were not the answer? We knew one thing—we had friends who believed Christ, and they were helping and supporting us. On that basis alone we stuck it out.

It is exactly twenty years since that all took place, and I have forgotten the names of the people who were so critical of us. Russ and I deliberately wiped that out of our minds—we had to in order to keep our balance spiritually and emotionally. We kept going to Sunday school and church, and if there were hard glances in our direction, I've forgotten that too. In fact I remember very little of those days except what concerned Carole Ann and Donna immediately.

There are times when the most constructive thing one can do is to forget what has been said or done. Remembering does no good, if it brings anger and hurt and frustration with it. In our reading we had come across the verse in Isaiah where God says, "I, even I, am he that blotteth out thy transgressions for mine own sake, and will not remember thy sins." If God chooses deliberately to forget what he might well bring up against us, then, we reasoned, we can do the same thing. We can decide to forget. And we did. It was not out of great spiritual maturity that we were able to put some painful memories out of our minds, but because we had to survive emotionally. When the pressure is so great, to some extent one's natural instinct goes to work, and the unbearable is buried in the subconscious.

Now that those events are a part of the distant past, when nothing is remembered emotionally, only intellectually, I can see that we were not strong enough then—perhaps no one ever is—to have made it on our own.

Our church supported us in two ways, and we needed both of them. It helped us officially, with money from the Board of Deacons tactfully and generously given. We appreciated this help immensely. But if the official help and sympathy had been all we received, it wouldn't have been enough to help us bear the weight of trouble. The best efforts of the church as an institution won't do what individual believers can do "to bear one another's burdens." Official expressions of sympathy, wonderful as they are, do not convey the sense of being cared about that one single Christian can give with nothing more than a handclasp.

We live in a country so immense that much of life is carried on in an institutional manner. There is help for those who need it financially, there are agencies in the multiplied hundreds whose job is to meet the needs of the people. They can do much. But there is one thing they will never be able to do, and that is to give one the sense of being a *person* cared for and valued by another person. In the light of the best our various institutions can do, a needy person is a project. And no one can bear the pressures and tensions of life knowing that he is nothing more than a project.

The church, part of our vastness in these United States, can't help being a big institution, too. But we Christians must keep it from being only that. The church is meant to be the visible expression of the love of God in the world. People need people. We as the Church were meant to function primarily as people. All the organizational structures that are needed to keep things going in this complex society we live in must never be allowed to get in the way of the primary goal Christ gave us—to be his people in his world.

In our case, we *did* receive help and sympathy from other Christians. People whom we knew only by name wrote telling us they cared about us and were praying for us. We received letters from others we didn't know giving encouragement and offers of help. We felt that the concern expressed by the church as an institution was genuine because the same concern came to us from individuals in the church.

It was Christ's people, giving Russ and me their individual time and concern and help that brought us through those hard, hard days. And that has been the story ever since. It is, I am convinced, the most natural way the Christian faith is propagated. We can only give others what has been given us. A large part of the faith Russ and I were learning to live was being given to us by the lives of our friends.

The love and sympathy of other Christians and particularly the help of our friends gradually turned our attention away from the anger and bitterness that some Christians had displayed. But newcomers to the Christian community will always tend to be taken aback, as Russ and I were, at finding that Christians aren't all perfect. Somehow we do expect Christians to be better than other people. Through the years, however, we have discovered that even Jesus Christ did not expect this to be true. We began to understand from our experience what he was talking about in one of his parables which he said was about "the kingdom of Heaven."

A farmer, he said, sowed "good seed" in a field that belonged to him. "But while his men were asleep his enemy came and sowed weeds among the wheat, and went away. When the crop came up and ripened, the weeds appeared as well. . . ." When the farmhands discovered the weeds they were upset and anxiously asked the farmer whether they shouldn't pull up the weeds. No, the farmer said; pulling up the weeds would uproot the wheat as well. They should just leave both to grow until the harvest. Then the wheat would be reaped and they could cull out and burn the weeds.

Jesus' disciples who heard this parable were puzzled. They understood the farming application, but what did it have to do with them. Jesus told them, "The man who has ears should use them!" In other words, "Pay attention, this concerns you." The weeds, he said, were the children of the evil one, who got mixed in with the good seed—the children of the kingdom.

As I think about Jesus' parable and about our experience, I realize that the weeds will always cause comment as not belonging in a wheat field. And I remember another of Jesus' parables in which he describes the varying yields that different heads of wheat produce—some give only a 30% yield, while others give 80% or even 100%.

In the Christian community the good lives, like the good wheat, do a great deal to cancel out the damage done by the others who have gotten mixed in, and by the non-producers. In times of crisis, when we get hurt by life and find that even in the church there are nettles that sting us, the wound can be eased and the pain relieved by the help that comes from God's ordinary Christians. They become a balm for the bruised, a weapon against evil, a defense against the attrition of our faith by the uncertainties and anxieties of life.

VIII

FRIENDSHIP

AND

FOIBLES

THE YEARS following that dreadful summer of 1948 were hard and often painful for our family. In spite of the tremendous help given by the National Foundation for the victims of polio, we were financially pressed because of the long period of treatment that followed the girls' hospitalization. Donna had very few aftereffects, but Carole Ann suffered from weakness in her abdominal muscles, as well as other residual effects. I spent much of my time driving the girls to the Childrens Hospital for therapy.

When Richard Halverson came to the church as one of the ministers, we asked him to teach a Bible study group. His teaching made all the difference in all our lives, and the bonds that were formed during those years have never weakened. Dick taught other groups also, and his ministry among us all as teacher and friend made an indelible imprint on our lives—for good.

Some years later, when Dick left the church to work with International Christian Leadership, and eventually to become minister to the Fourth Presbyterian Church in Washington, D.C., another Richard came to be a minister on our staff. Dr. Richard Langford began to teach the Homebuilders class, and to become a friend. I saw something in his life I had seen in Dick Halverson's life, and I am sure it exists in the life of every minister—the quality of patience.

Patience is especially necessary for a teacher or leader because without it he will soon tire of the stupidity, the lack of sensitivity, and the spiritual torpor his flock will display. We are not brighter, or quicker, or better than other people just because we are Christians. We have simply recognized the fact that we are sinners and that Christ has redeemed us. Sometimes there is a great gap between that experience and any growth at all.

The need for patience doesn't stop with leaders, however.

There is a lot of talk today about "hang-ups," a catchy phrase for a condition humans have always lived with: sin. I know that the word "sin" is very unfashionable at the moment, but it is one of the major facts of life. We are sinful people, who begin the Christian life with some areas of life more infected by sin than others. We can cope with certain problems, but others defeat us entirely—those blind spots and stubborn places in our personalities where attitudes have crystallized so that change is very difficult.

All of this means that we will rub on one another at times,

we will irritate one another, and most serious of all, we will resist teaching which hits us at these sensitive areas, the places we've built a wall around because they are so tender.

The sooner we each learn how important it is to have patience, the more easily will our relationships with each other function smoothly. Since we all have different problems, or hang-ups, or sensitive areas—whatever one wants to term our human fallibility and foibles—we need patience so we will be able to live and work with people whose hang-ups are different than ours. It would be ideal if we were all so understanding and sensitive about problems we ourselves don't have that we just overflowed with love and acceptance. But we are not living in an ideal situation, and we are not ideal people.

We also need patience for society's problems. We are tempted to think that all problems can be resolved, all unhappy situations changed for good because we have been able to make such giant strides in many fields. Technology is a wonderful aid to a better life, but it is not the ultimate answer. There are some human dilemmas no technological advances will ever do away with. If we abolish all poverty, all illiteracy, all race prejudice, we will still have human ills. Being human, which means being sinful, we will create new problems.

We all become impatient with the slowness of social changes which seem to us to be obviously needed; but we ourselves are part of the slowdown, because every one of us has certain areas in which we resist change. Our impatience is the most frustrating attitude we can have, because nothing will ever change enough to keep pace with our demands.

One can understand how non-Christians, who have no world view except the rather general idea that we can conquer man's social and moral problems exactly as we are conquering physical problems, might become impatient. They see the urgency of the need and are in a hurry.

Many Christians are quick to chide these idealists for their impatience. We remind them (needlessly, since they do not accept our basic premise that God is sovereign) that God moves slowly to accomplish his will. The ironic factor in our position is that while we are viewing social situations with complacency, accepting certain evils in society as inevitable because of man's sinfulness and asking the world to wait while God and his Church work slowly to make men better, we frequently have an entirely different viewpoint when the situation becomes personal.

Such people were Russ and I in those years of personal trial. We knew there was suffering in the world; we could see quite clearly how impossible it was for God to right ancient wrongs overnight. *But* when it came to our own troubles, we complained and whined and writhed in impatience.

We had to learn the lesson of patience during the difficult years following the girls' illness, and we were helped because our friends were patient with us. There were times when our tempers were frayed, times when we were not cheerful company and they might easily have left us out. After all, a dinner party is not exactly helped by guests who are tense and distraught with worries. Their forbearance, however, was getting through to us, and when we were able to see beyond our own noses, when the preoccupation with our own troubles began to disappear, we realized that nothing but the love of Christ could have kept our friends with us.

We remembered what Dick Halverson had said to us about our need to wait for God, and we began to see that we were impatient people—impatient in the most devastating way of all, impatient with God!

Our friends had been patient with us, that we knew well. Now we saw that their patience was a godly patience, and that behind them, beyond them, above them, loomed the God of the universe, bearing patiently with us while we chafed, and complained, and strained with impatience. This truth was of the greatest magnitude in changing our lives for the better. I believe that the quality of patience with friends, with children, with business and associates and people generally, is essential to getting along happily in this world—but above all, to getting along with God.

To be impatient with God, chronically, habitually impatient with him because things are not to our liking, makes the Christian life a dreadful burden. He will not change his timetable to suit us, he is not going to adapt his program in the world to our every whim; he is not going to do for us what we ought to do for ourselves. One of the hard facts about life is that nothing here is perfect. God is not going to make it so because we demand it of him.

Another hard fact is that in this sinful world, muddling along its own way and oblivious to God, things will not always go well with Christians. We are *in* the world, not above it; and we are involved in all that happens, good or bad, just like everyone else. We get sick because there is disease and Christians are not exempt; we have accidents because they happen, and we are not miraculously delivered; we have money troubles because people do foolish things, or because they are dishonest, and we are sometimes the victims of our own folly and sometimes the victims of others' dishonesty. There is nothing in this world that we have been excused from, nothing at all.

The patience—or forbearance—which we were learning was necessary to ease the little strains of life as well as to

survive the big ones. The minor irritations are part of living
for all of us. For instance, I find it much easier to tolerate
certain traits than others, and much patience is needed when
I am with someone whose little oddities are not *my* little
oddities. All of life involves getting along with people, and
inevitably, getting along with all sorts of people different than
we are.

The need for patience was graphically illustrated by a situation in our family when the children were growing up.
Russ was very good at mathematics. He could not understand
that for me the entire area was a mystery I had never pene-
trated. He was fairly patient with my shortcomings because
he realized that I had lived nineteen years of my life before
I met him, nineteen years of determined ignorance as far as
mathematics was concerned. It was one of my hang-ups. But
when it came to our children, he decided that if they started
right they could learn mathematics properly; anyone with
ordinary intelligence could. I knew all that, and I knew I
had a mental block on the whole matter. What neither of
us knew was that somehow or other, one never quite under-
stands how these things come about, *none* of our children
would be particularly brilliant in the field of mathematics,
and one of them (Donna) would catch, by osmosis presumably,
my deplorable attitude.

When she was in high school Donna got a D in a math
class, and Russ tried working with her. Her inability to comprehend what seemed to him to be crystal clear produced
that kind of tension all parents know about—when one's voice
grows louder and a strident note begins to appear, when the
son or daughter gets teary-eyed and trembly, and—well, you
know how it all ends. Donna wept, Russ fumed, and then
was so sorry for her he apologized. After the storm was over,

we all decided he'd better not try to help her any more, he hadn't the patience.

I mention this incident because we all have had similar experiences—either being the one who can't understand and begins to crack under the strain of demands too much for one's poor brain, or of trying to explain the matter slowly and clearly, going over and over it and ending up by shouting. Ethel May Baldwin, who is the Administrative Assistant in Christian Education at the First Presbyterian Church of Hollywood, once put her finger on the heart of the matter: "The essence of good teaching is being able to tell someone the same thing over and over and over again, without implying that they have ever heard it before and are stupid for not knowing it." Teachers *must* have that quality, as must pastors and Christian leaders. Parents must develop it, if they don't have it to begin with, or they will make a fine mess of their children's lives. And friends must have it for each other.

As we become aware that we *are* learning to be more patient or loving or kind or thoughtful there is always the temptation to think, "There, now, that's enough. I've learned my lesson," and expect to be through with the instructive (but difficult) problems. Just as we were congratulating ourselves that the hard places we'd gone through had served their purpose and, we hoped, life might ease up a little, all we had known of patience and trust and faith in God was needed. We were faced with the unavoidable question, "Is your patience—your love for God—your trust in him—enough when death comes?"

IX
JUST
BEING
THERE

TO ONE who believes in nothing but this life, death *is* the final catastrophe, the one evil which must, at all costs, be put off as long as possible.

At this point it would be interesting to explore a little more profoundly the connection between modern man's fear of death and his tolerance of any condition, any evil, any degradation, even slavery, rather than resist. Resistance means war, war means killing, killing means death—and death is the end of everything. The almost universal cry for Peace and Freedom (though they are not necessarily synonymous or always compatible) can be understood once we see that *anything* to the modern pagan is better than death—that is, extinction.

To Christians, death is the fundamental test of one's faith. For Russ and me its immediacy forced us to evaluate everything we believed. It is possible to put off all the final, hard, determinative questions of life until they touch us personally; then one must face them. Either the Christian gospel is true, and makes death no longer fearsome or death makes nonsense of our faith. Russ and I did make that evaluation. We were forced to it by circumstances. But I do not believe we would have had the stamina to come through and *think* through and live through what we had to face without our friends.

Late in 1950 Carole Ann began to show some new weaknesses. There followed a long period of testing, of diagnoses, of therapy, of alternate periods of hope and despair, and eventually of the chill conviction that whatever the diagnosis said, she had something wrong with her far worse than we knew. I am not a person given to flashes of insight, nor visions, nor special spiritual experiences. But during those months the conviction seized me (seized is not too strong a word) that Carole Ann was going to die.

I was fragmented inside by grief and anger at God, by sudden short-lived periods of hopefulness, by a dreadful horror that this all had come upon us because of my lack of faith in God. I had heard so much about the "prayer of faith" and how God works in direct proportion to our faith (which does not seem to be a clear-cut New Testament concept) that I was afraid that whatever was wrong with Carole Ann was my fault. If only I could believe God would heal her! I struggled to make myself believe. I prayed and wept, and then in the fatigue of overdrawn emotions felt desolate and alone.

I found myself unable to discuss this with Russ. How does

one say to one's husband, "Dear, I think that in spite of all the encouragement the doctor has given us, Carole Ann is going to die"? We were walled off from each other by our mutual fear.

Opal and John Hughes, whom we had known for several years, along with other friends, were our source of strength and comfort. When I could bear the agony of my own turmoil and fears no longer, I usually called Opal. I do not remember any of our conversations, I only remember that they were, for me, the strength and help I needed. I knew she cared about our family, and about Carole Ann, and I knew that when I was too tired and discouraged to pray, she prayed.

In the end, we discovered that Carole Ann had an inoperable brain tumor. After an exploratory operation to see what was there, they simply told us there was no hope. She lived in a deep coma for two weeks and then died. But by then, we had already come to a resting place of trust in God. All the months preceding the surgery when I had fought the battle with God, when I had flung my arguments and reproaches at him as I went about my housework with desperate intensity, were the months of crucial decision.

I remember one night, just before the surgery, when Russ and I in the numbness of intolerable grief knelt by our bed and told God that Carole Ann was his and we trusted him, but we certainly didn't understand what he was doing. It was capitulation to God—no triumphal rising above tragedy, no glorious outburst of faith; but it was still faith. We could not comprehend why Carole Ann had to die, but we could not escape the conviction that God was there, that he would take care of Carole Ann in death as well as in life.

While she lay in the hospital, our friends were there with us. Early in the morning, late at night, all during the day

The Many Faces Of Friendship

they came and sat with us. We didn't have to talk, we didn't have to do anything. They were just there with us. That was the very thing we needed most. We didn't need to have the theology of suffering and death explained to us; that was for us to think through, with the Bible, for ourselves. We didn't need to be exhorted to stand firm in the faith, or to have Scripture verses quoted to us. We simply needed to be *cared* for, to be with our friends, to be not alone.

Really, that is what we needed most from God. We had to come to the recognition of our own fallibility, our limited comprehension, and accept the fact that we did not then and will never in this life understand events and circumstances and the twists and bends of history. We simply needed to know that God cared for us, and that we were not lost strangers in an unfriendly universe.

The reassurance that we are important to God, that he cares for us—that he even shares our human nature—is exactly what we are given in the incarnation. Jesus Christ came to make restitution for the wrongness of the world, for the wrongness of human nature—to die for our sins, to use the familiar phrase. But he did more than just make right what had gone wrong. He also came to show us what God is like. At the same time he showed us what man can be like when he is in harmony with God. He also showed us man as he ought to be in action.

We know a lot about God from the Old Testament: that he is holy, righteous, ablaze with perfection; powerful, personal—interested in his poor foolish creatures. We know all of this, but we don't know, until we *see* Jesus Christ as the Son of God, that his forgiveness is greater than our sins, that he accepts us when we come to him with our soiled lives, and that there is no end to his mercy. Even if Jesus had never worked one miracle, or healed one leper, just his coming to be one of us would have given us the assurance we needed so desperately—the assurance that God is concerned with our lives.

We'll never see another man like Jesus Christ until we see one another transformed in another dimension. Our ineradicable human tendency toward sin has made that vision quite impossible now. But we have seen what God *meant,* when he made man—just as we have seen God's attitude toward us in Jesus Christ.

Every time someone is unhappy and lonely because of the sickness and tragedy and death this world lives in, that person needs to know God is with him. There is nothing greater, nothing more spiritual or more helpful that anyone can do than to do what our friends did—simply come and be with us in our sorrow.

There are two other ways in which people treat the sorrows of their fellows, and neither one does any good. Those without faith or whose faith is too nebulous to be of any good at such a time usually stay away from someone who is seriously ill, facing death, or who has had a death in the family. They don't know what to say, and feel the awkwardness of their inability to give comfort or help so they just stay away. Christians, on the other hand, frequently feel called upon to go to someone in such dire trouble and give them (1) a little homily on the necessity for trusting God, (2) some pious phrases about how glorious it is to be in heaven with Christ, or, (3) a run-through of Biblical teaching on eternal life, just to make sure one's faith doesn't give out. This is perhaps the cruelest blow of all at such a time.

Faith isn't strengthened by lectures on the subject, or by a theological explanation of sin, suffering and death. It is built up *by one thing,* aside from the work of the Holy Spirit inwardly—by the love and concern of other Christians. Our friends acted out, so to speak, the love of God for us in being with us, in being sensitive to our needs and, most of all, in their awareness and acceptance of the fact that sorrow and loss are real.

No matter how sure our faith in eventual triumph over death, how certain we are that the ones we have loved are with Christ, when they are gone life here is different. Nothing will ever be quite the same. That is not to say life won't be good, but it will be different. The empty place left by one person, unique and unlike any other being on earth, is never filled in this life. To understand that and accept it, and not try and gloss it over, is the beginning of spiritual maturity.

How fortunate we were to have friends who knew that! They knew that there would never be another Carole Ann, that we needed strength for today, not encouragement for heaven. Heaven was no problem to us—it was how to get along in this life until we get there.

I am absolutely certain in my own mind that it is necessary to know the truth, to know what the Bible has to say, and to have a firm foundation in the Scriptures. I am equally sure that we will never *really* be quite sure of our faith until it is tested, and until we see it lived out in human lives. The two go together, and make the gospel of Christ believable.

X

LIFELINE
TO
SANITY

IN THE YEARS following the death of Carole Ann there were some changes in our lives that come to nearly all of us sooner or later. We moved. Not just from one part of the city to the other, or even to a different part of the state; but to a different part of the country. The move was very difficult for me, as I get my roots down very deep and feel a strong sense of security in having a home in one place.

No doubt all sorts of interesting speculations could be entered into here. We hate change (many of us) because we are insecure, and we are insecure because we are not yet "at home" in the universe—that will only come with Heaven.

The Many Faces Of Friendship

Or, we are always trying to find some kind of lasting safety here on earth (a stable home, old friends, familiar places) which we can never really have in this life. These things are true, I know—but all the same, there it is. Some of us move happily and easily across the country, make new friends, adjust to new surroundings—and some of us don't.

Our move to a Midwestern state, coming in 1952 at the end of five years of illness, financial distress, worry, and finally the death of a child, was too much for me. I began to have a nervous breakdown.

Although I had come to a kind of exhausted trust in God when Carole Ann died, it was not a once-and-forever decision. It never is. We are not made of metal or stone so that our attitudes are unchanging, but of thoughts and emotions as fluid as a river. Trust, once affirmed, has to be renewed. The determination to do a good deed or make the right decision must be made each time action is called for.

God was there, I knew, but what were his intentions toward me? I knew already he would not spare me any of the sorrows the human race experiences. Did he intend for me to be happy at all? The very look of the strange countryside depressed me.

The depression deepened, and was darkened by nameless fears. I awoke every morning in an unreasoning fright, and it grew worse as the day went on. I could not handle the situation. We were in a strange city and a strange church with no one to turn to. In the end, we moved back to California, to Hollywood.

It all sounds so simple. At the time it was so involved and so agonizing. Russ was leaving what looked like a promising career with an oil company. Moving home did not automatically make me well, it never does. I did not have a nervous breakdown, but not having it was nearly as devastating as if I had. I did not, at that time, know a Christian psychologist (since then several people in that field have become friends) and I was overwhelmed with guilt and shame. Russ and I had taken in, almost by osmosis, the hazy but very prevalent idea that if one's relationship to Christ is all right, then there will be no troubles, mental, spiritual or moral, that we cannot "have the victory" over. There will be no temptations we cannot overcome (I read I Corinthians 10:13 over and over again), and surely giving way to an emotional breakdown would be the same as being overcome by temptation.

I had arrived at the conclusion slowly and through painful consideration, that God does not spare us physical or financial troubles, or the accidents mankind is prone to. Yet the prevailing attitude that we are safe from inner fears and turmoils, whatever other ills may befall us from outside, had made its mark. I could understand that one is not responsible for cancer, or unforeseen accident, or the like—but I really believed that if I were spiritually "right" then I would be right emotionally and mentally.

That, of course, all took place more than fifteen years ago. The climate of thinking in this country, even in the most sheltered evangelical circles, has changed greatly since then. From attributing all problems and emotional troubles to sin, or lack of trust in Christ, we have gotten so preoccupied with psychology that we now are tempted to lay all sin at the door of some psychological aberration for which one is not responsible. I do not think this is a healthy, or correct point of view any more than my oversimplified view of the "victorious Christian life" was healthy or correct.

At any rate, I knew no professional to turn to except the pastor I was closest to, Dick Halverson. He reassured me, and helped me, and tried to understand my terrors. But he was beset by people, and I couldn't always talk to him when I was clinging to balance. I talked to a friend.

I may say right now that I am sure it is far better (and kinder to one's friends) to go immediately to a qualified Christian counselor, a psychiatrist or psychologist. But there wasn't one available. Russ and I were far from being able to afford a psychiatrist's fees, and I had enough objectivity left to try to make it on my own. I did not, of course. No one ever makes it on his own. I made it, by God's grace, and because of his grace, and primarily because he gave me one friend to whom I could talk. Opal Hughes was literally my lifeline during those dark months. I know that without her sane, balanced, yet never disinterested nor judgmental counsel, I would indeed have had a very serious breakdown.

It took months, even years, before I was really over it; and the whole of the miserable episode can be capsuled in this sentence: I finally realized that there were two possibilities—either the Bible was true or it was not. If it was not, everyone was in the soup and there was no help for me; if it was true, then all the promises of God's care and concern and keeping power were true, *whether I felt like it or not.* I simply could not bring myself to believe, even in my most desperate moments, that the Bible was not true. All the evidence of my life to that time pointed the other way—to its reliability. In the end, ten minutes at a time, I clung to that belief that God was for me, even when I felt most abandoned.

It's all past now, and I've talked over enough of my life with friends in the field of psychology so that I understand the tensions and pressures that brought me to the edge of despair. Now I can say, "Yes, I see—because *that* happened long ago, and I reacted *this* way, then such a happening was inevitable." But that is not the important thing.

What *is* important is that it was a friend who made the difference in my life. Not my husband—he was too concerned, too anxious to be helpful. Not my church—I was too embarrassed to let anyone know what I was going through for fear they would think there must be something wrong with my spiritual life. Dick and Doris Halverson were towers of strength, and I needed their help, but that would not have done it alone. No minister can take on such a burden, unless he does nothing other than counseling. Opal took the burden, and kept me from going under.

The other day I asked her how she could have stood the pressure of my need. She replied that she remembered the time before I had begun to go to pieces, and knew that this trouble was temporary and the time would come again when I was a whole person. What faith! My own faith in God was, I am sure, built up and sustained by her faith.

There are people all around us, people whom we meet every day, who need the understanding, sympathetic ear of a friend. True, many of them are too disturbed to be helped much by anyone but a professional counselor, but I am quite sure, from what others have told me since that time, that most of us *at some time in our lives* can be kept from an emotional disaster by the help of a friend, or friends.

This does not mean that to give such help one ought to be oozing sympathy and concern and pity. Far from it. A matter-of-fact appraisal of the situation is far better. Opal sometimes told me that what I needed was to put my mind deliberately on something constructive; and I did just that. If I hadn't, of course, even her help would not have availed.

Dealing with a tendency to be depressed is, in one sense, exactly like dealing with any other disagreeable fact of life—like resentment (which we discussed in the last chapter).

Stop thinking about it and think about something positive. Friends who are willing to be honest and tell one when it is time to use some self-discipline are the best friends there are.

A great deal is required of the one who is ready to be that kind of friend; it costs to be involved in someone else's life and troubles. Sensitivity is needed, and an ability to put the truth in words that are neither too harsh nor too soothing to be heard. Finally, one must be aware of the time when help can become damaging instead of uplifting. We all have a little bit of the "leaner" in us, and some people will lean forever if you let them. Always calling for help, always asking for sympathy, always demanding time—but never ever doing anything they are advised to do, nor taking any steps toward helping themselves. That was not my particular temptation, because I am an activist by nature; my first impulse is to do something—anything, even the wrong thing—to straighten out a bad situation. For the person who is passive, however, the danger is very real and very deadly. It's so easy to become problem oriented; to adjust to having difficulties, to discuss them endlessly, to be forever delving into one's own interior to see what can be dredged up.

There comes a time, no matter how deep the problems are or how serious the consequences, when one must stop talking and start coping. Belief, in the Biblical sense, means living the way you think. Once assent has been given to the truth of a situation, it must be put into action or it is not really belief at all. The whole spring of Christian action lies in the principle that we act upon our faith. An acting brings change.

Some change we don't like—the passing away of good times, of happy situations. But the Christian life has also a good kind of change. Things can be better; we can alter the situation for good. God has chosen to act through us, his children, and his will is not accomplished without our participation. Action, to be constructive, means self-discipline. My parents had schooled me well in that, and I was able because of discipline and the very real help of a friend, not to go under.

There were other ways in which help came to me. Our first Sunday home from the Midwest a new minister preached his first sermon in our church. It was some time before Russ and I came to know Dr. Raymond Lindquist as a friend, but from the beginning his sermons gave me strength to keep going.

"You know," he told me once when we were discussing a sermon of his I had found particularly helpful, "when the New Testament says, 'All things work together for good to them that love God,' the 'all things' includes *us*."

That is what has happened to me. I am not merely on the receiving end of life, but involved in the working out of God's good plan. And so are my friends. I have found that Ray's sermons are given life and meaning by friends. Paul was talking about this kind of involvement when he wrote, "You are an open letter about Christ which we ourselves have written, not with pen and ink but with the Spirit of the living God. Our message has been engraved not in stone, but in living men and women."

XI

THE QUALITIES OF FRIENDSHIP

SOME PEOPLE are always searching for friends, always lurking pathetically around the fringes of a group, never really one of the group, never quite at ease nor quite comfortable. They are so pitiable in their obvious longing for acceptance that everyone feels, uneasily, that it would be uncharitable and unkind, even unchristian, not to do everything possible to make them feel welcome.

Whatever gestures toward friendship and acceptance are made, and ostensibly received, the relationship with such a person remains hollow. There is no substance to it, nothing to make it more than a superficial exchange of pleasantries.

After awhile the mechanics of artificial enthusiasm and interest become fatiguing, and the attempt to foster a friendship dwindles away. Why? Why are there some unhappy souls who never have any friends at all?

All of us have known many of these people. We always feel half guilty because we can't summon up more enthusiasm for their company. Yet they have the same effect on nearly everyone. They are, in some indefineable manner, repellant.

To have friends one must be a friend, and some people never understand what it means to be a friend. In *The Four Loves*, C. S. Lewis says that friendship is always *about* something. It does not happen in a vacuum. Erotic attraction between a man and a woman can flare like a sudden spark entirely apart from any common interest. Indeed, it can be present when there is absolutely nothing but its own magnetism to draw two people together—no similarity of background, no common viewpoint, nothing to make a relationship have content except the attraction itself.

Friendship is not like that. There must be something other than a mutual spark of liking to keep the relationship going. Lovers can be absorbed in each other, or in the effect the other has on one's own self, which is really self-absorption. Friends, however, don't sit around and talk endlessly about the friendship; they have to have something outside each other for the friendship to feed on.

It has seemed to me that the people who never succeed in making friends are people who haven't any content to offer a friendship. They have nothing to give: no interest in anything to contribute, no project, or ideas, or purpose about which friendships can be formed. They are simply there, empty, waiting to be filled.

This viewpoint about friendship has come rather slowly.

Russ and I realized the change that had taken place in our own lives as we progressed from being nominal Christians to serious, committed Christians. We had had friends before, and the friendship was about something—Russ's work, a mutual interest, even a liking for playing pinochle. The relationships never went very deep because our common interests were so ephemeral.

We continued to have, and I still have, friends who do not share my Christian convictions; but most of them are people who think seriously about life, so that there is something for us to build our friendship around even though we don't agree about some things. The other casual friendships dropped away, and so shallow was the impression they had made that we hardly noticed their passing. Many of our deepest, most lasting friendships were formed with Christians, which seems quite natural since our relationship was built upon the source of all reality, Christ.

As these friendships grew, especially in the years following Carole Ann's death, we were learning how to be friends. We were beginning to understand that not only were our relationships built on a mutual faith in Christ, and an affinity of personality and temperament, but that we could, indeed we must, make a contribution to the friendship, have something of interest to add to the relationship.

There are two extremes to sharing one's interests. One is seen in the person who answers questions politely with a "Yes" or "No" answer, and goes no further. After awhile the conversation lags, because most of us get tired of asking questions and getting nothing but monosyllables back; it makes one feel like a human True or False examination.

At the other end of the spectrum is the enthusiastic person who launches into a detailed exposition of his or her particular project in life and can never be turned off. There is no conversation, only a monologue. My son once said of such a person, "He's always speaking from the platform no matter where he is." Somewhere between the two extremes there is a balance. At that point of balance the most stimulating friendships can be found.

In addition to this, Russ and I learned more surely every day that to have friends one must make sacrifices. I cannot have friendship on *my* terms alone. To be a friend means to be willing to suffer inconvenience in order to help someone else. It means taking time to talk to someone when there is work you'd rather be doing, or a book you'd rather be reading, or a schedule that isn't being met. It means accepting responsibility, being able to respond to overtures of friendship with similar gestures. Most of all, it means abandoning self-centeredness and turning our attention to the needs of others.

Notice I did not say we ought to give up being selfish. Simple, uncomplicated selfishness is much easier to put up with than self-centeredness. C. S. Lewis pointed out that quite generous people have been, and are, self-centered; their trouble lies not in being selfish but in intense concentration on themselves, so that even their virtues (which they talk about and display conspicuously) exist and are used for their own satisfaction. Such people make poor friends, and usually don't succeed in having good friendships, because they demand constant attention and admiration.

Some potential friendships never materialize; they are pushed away. From time to time I have recoiled from someone who wanted to be my friend because she obviously wanted to be my only friend. When someone begins to show signs of jealousy of my other friendships or to monopolize my time, I beat a rapid retreat. Genuine friendship is not exclusive.

The Qualities Of Friendship

These qualifications for friendship which we were learning are attitudes which lead one to the final lesson to be learned; we must give up our right to be offended or hurt or to cling to resentment when we are wounded. This is a goal, or an ideal toward which we are traveling, although none of us has arrived. More and more, however, its primacy grows in my own thinking. To be so *un*self-centered that one can forget (not merely forgive) careless words and offenses, even deliberate injuries which are meant to lacerate, is not natural. All that is human in me rises up in wrath and indignation at such times. I really understand the phrase, "my blood boiled," because that's exactly how I feel when I'm hurt by someone.

And yet—human though it may be to respond or react instinctively in wounded anger, to retort in kind—it's not Christian. Nothing in the Christian life is natural, or instinctive. That fact is one of those truths I find hard to accept, and I suspect it is hard for us all. Every one of us has a secret hope that God will somehow either remake our natures so that goodness is effortless, or accommodate his demands to our faultiness. That's why so many Christians discount, or ignore, the Sermon on the Mount; it makes no concessions at all to our tendency to bite and scratch and kick (metaphorically speaking), and demands instead that we bring our lives into conformity with the kingdom of Heaven, where another standard prevails.

What I have come to, slowly and stumblingly through the years, and what I achieve only spasmodically and imperfectly, is the realization that these stringent spiritual and ethical demands which seem so impossible are necessary for any kind of happiness at all in life. Jesus knew very well we wouldn't arrive at perfection. He also knew what we find out painfully and through hard experience—that unless we *try*, unless we

97

give ourselves in genuine commitment to his rule in our lives, which is the same thing as saying we accept the Sermon on the Mount as reasonable and worth attempting to live by, we will be miserable, disappointed and frustrated people.

When he said, "Love your enemies, and pray for those who persecute you," he was merely telling us to do what will, in the long run, bring happiness. Everyone you know will be your enemy at some time—when he hurts you, or slights you, or takes sides against you. Father, mother, friends, sisters and brothers, children (these most of all) become, in our eyes, enemies at times. Retaliation is fatal, for it deepens the enmity; wrong has been answered with wrong, and there is no end to that dreary road. Someone, somewhere along the line, has to reverse the process, has to do the painful but necessary deed of offering forgiveness and a willingness to forget.

I have written about how Russ and I did manage to forget some wounds when we were hurt by criticism and anger toward us at the time our daughters had polio. That was possible only because God gave us grace in a measure we normally don't have, and because we were sustained and encouraged by our friends. But friends, however genuine and kind and wonderful they are, may sometimes offend. Even though they do it unwittingly, we tend to react with resentment.

At such times we need to call on all that we have of the grace of God, to remember all Jesus said about forgiveness, and to *immediately* put our minds to other things. There's no good in thinking about a painful incident and trying to forgive; it can't be done, at least not until the memory fades into paler colors. The only sensible remedy for such wounds is, first, to pray and spell out to God exactly how hurt, angry, and perhaps how right we feel ourselves to be. He may, at that point, remind us of incidents in the past where we have been the one giving offense; that does a great deal to put the sin against us in proper perspective. He may cause us to think twice about just exactly how right our position is, and to modify our thinking and admit our position to be less impregnable than we thought. Whatever conclusions one comes to, the next thing, and the vital thing, is to stop dwelling on the offense, to be busy with other concerns.

By doing this, two very good objectives are achieved. It's far easier to let one's sensibilities be soothed and calmed when the irritant is not always present at the surface of the consciousness. Being busy with other matters must necessarily give an interest, a content to life; and no friendship is possible without content.

It's quite revealing to me that many of the people I observe failing to make good friendships are people who are preoccupied with themselves, and often present a rather aggrieved appearance; they are all ready to be offended, indeed they seem to expect it, and respond instantly to any real or imagined slight.

My friends put up with a lot from me. I often say things that (to my horror) come out sounding very different than I had intended them to. Usually it's far worse to try and explain than it is to simply drop the subject and count on Christian mercy. I get absent-minded, and forget to speak to people; this happens frequently because I am a member of a very large church and see the same people several times in the course of a week, sometimes several times a day. I don't always "see" them when I'm hurrying and preoccupied. If they were not kind and forgiving, they could be hurt with me nearly all the time.

The least I can do, therefore, is to give my utmost to be

as understanding as those around me. It would be unreasonable for me to expect others to know how inoffensive my intentions are, even when I say something awkward or unfortunate, and at the same time be quick to take offense. Spiritual laws work in all situations, they are never suspended for our convenience. Jesus pointed this out when he said, "For if you forgive other people their failures, your Heavenly Father will also forgive you. But if you will not forgive other people, neither will your Heavenly Father forgive you your failures."

When we let resentment and hurt and anger build up inside, they take up so much space there's no room even for the forgiveness of God. It isn't that he won't forgive us—it's that he can't, when we are unforgiving. When we are at peace and happy with God, a climate of love and forbearance toward others is produced. When we allow ourselves to be ruffled and resentful toward others, our relationship with Christ deteriorates.

It may be that you've known this and practiced it for years, or that you were fortunate enough to be gifted with a happy and uncomplicated temperament which just isn't sensitive to the situations that irritate and offend most of us. If so, you may thank God for such a golden gift. But if you are like me, irritable by nature, take heart. God will never give up on us. His grace is available in unending abundance.

XII
SEEING
EYE
TO
EYE

IT TAKES all kinds to make a world, people say frequently; but many of us have a private sequel to that old saying. Under our breath we add, "But *my* kind is best."

Why do we so often insist that our friends think on all issues exactly as we do? Why are we so uncomfortable with people of different political convictions, different shades of religious opinion, different ideas of what is good art, or music, or literature?

It's easy, of course, to be relaxed and comfortable among those with whom there is some shared interest or concern; but to insist that our families and friends think just as we do on every conceivable subject is ridiculous. Yet such insistence is common among Christians. Some of us have even narrowed our horizons so that we exclude other Christians whose form of worship, or creed, or confession does not square in every detail with ours. The natural human tendency to be exclusive when spiritualized negates the very faith we hold.

The arrogance of such a stance is incompatible with any real understanding of Christ and what he came to do; it makes critics of the church out of those who might otherwise see the Christian faith as a possible option. Such rigidity of thought has a blighting effect on all relationships, making friendship difficult and alienating one's children. In fact, I've noticed more and more that life is very like a seamless web—the qualities which make for a good friend also make for good parents—and the opposite is equally true.

Although such reasoning sounds very wise and mature, it has only been in the last few years that I have come to see its validity and to put it into practice. I still find it difficult not to be rigid and probably always will. When we became Christians, Russ and I were just as opinionated, just as fearful of change and as suspicious of those whose way of living was different from ours as the most provincial hayseed. In fact, we *were* provincial. One of the good alterations a genuine Christian faith made in our lives was the broadening of our horizons making provinciality more and more impossible.

God's world is very big, far larger than any bit of it we will ever know; his mercy is wide, beyond our small comprehension. We began to open out to some of his largeness when we came to know Christ. The enchanting variety our friends provided widened the window still farther. We have found, too, that unless one is totally closed to all new thought, having children grow up and become individuals completes the job.

As Darrell brought home new ideas and new knowledge—especially during his college and seminary years—and
as Donna contributed her original thinking to our table talk,
Russ and I were learning. Although we didn't think it through
at the time, we were learning two things, both extremely
important: how to keep thinking and growing, avoiding
rigidity and crystallized opinions; and how to become friends
with our children.

Right now, talk about the generation gap is very big. Undoubtedly there is a gap. The very nature of life makes such
a gap inevitable. We can't limit ourselves to the way of thinking of twenty years ago (though it is possible to remember
and be understanding), and no contemporary young person
can think himself into our frame of reference—he hasn't the
material, the background and personal history, the recollec-
tions and experiences to work with. The gap is there. But
it needn't be impassable. It can be bridged in the same way
one narrows the chasm between people—proceding from acquaintance to friendship by acceptance of each other's
differences, and by some attempt to understand another's
viewpoint.

Recently I've been teaching a six-week seminar of high
school students in Sunday school. It's a discussion group on
practical Christianity in the family. I often find myself wishing
parents could hear their children as they discuss their attitudes
toward parents, the family, and their faith.

One of the attitudes children most resent in their parents
is a rigid demand for conformity. "I don't see how you can
stand that crazy music! Sounds like screeching to me; doesn't
even have a melody you can hum. Now take a good old song
like . . ." Or, "I don't care if everyone *is* wearing long side-
burns, you're going to get a haircut today! I won't have my

son looking like a hippie." "Do you mean to stand there and tell me the school *allows* girls to wear skirts that short?"

Whatever the subject of the disagreement, and however strongly parents may feel about the rightness of their position, an uncompromising attitude shuts off all possible communication. Most of the matters that are of concern between the generations are matters of custom, not of morals. It is obvious, however, that there is also a rebellion among the young generation as far as morals are concerned, and it is a shame to give them cause to believe that our convictions about the length of one's skirts, or one's hair, are of the same importance as our convictions about morality. That is exactly what many younger people conclude. Their parents get just as upset about the way their sons and daughters look as about matters of ethics.

This unbending demand for absolute conformity also shuts out those who might otherwise become good friends. We set up standards, decide they are God's standards, and then choose friends who fit the pattern. We are the poorer for it; and if, as is happening frequently today in Christian homes, we do the same with our children, we "turn them off." They then turn us off, and they turn off our faith, because to them our faith is synonymous with our way of eating, dressing, combing our hair, and dismissing what we don't agree with.

At an afternoon tea, I once listened to a woman complain about her daughter's current boy friend. "I do hope she doesn't get serious about him," said she, "he's a Lutheran." The lady sitting on my other side whispered, chuckling, "My daughter is married to a Lutheran minister."

In an entirely different group, one woman said to another, very darkly, "Whatever you do, don't join a Presbyterian Church. You know what *they* are!" Not being one to let such a thing go unchallenged, I said, "I am a Presbyterian. What are we?" It turned out that her concept of Presbyterians was based more on prejudice than knowledge—most such generalizations are.

Some of my friends vote the same political ticket I do, some don't. We discuss politics happily and without rancor, because we are all interested in our country and its welfare. Disagreements? Of course! But does that mean they must become personal? No.

There are two obvious reasons for accepting people of diverse viewpoints, both in our faith and in other matters. The first is that since none of us is infallible and has a corner on the truth, it just *may* be we don't know everything. God no doubt will correct much of our thinking when we get to heaven. The other is that since God has provided such an infinite variety in nature, and in human nature, presumably he likes variety and doesn't expect us to be cranked out of the same sausage machine. He could have made us all alike, but he chose not to. Instead he endowed us with individuality so marked by his own creativeness that each one of us is unique.

How foolish we are, then, not to happily accept this wonderful conglomeration of living human beings. Of course we will be more like some than others. Of course there are similarities and marks of identification within groups. But not *absolute* conformity, never that.

Variety within Christian unity is good and necessary. But not serious and permanent divisions. We Christians may not be complacent about our splits, our scandalous alienation from each other, by our arrogance which claims infallibility for our point of view and denies the brotherhood that is in Christ to those who disagree.

Writing to a faction-ridden church at Corinth, Paul pleaded with them not to be split into parties, but to be one in Christ. They were not to judge one another but to have patience and tolerance with their Christian brothers.

To the Romans Paul wrote about the ordinary matters of life—eating, drinking, and keeping holy days. His command was to abstain from criticising one another, since we all answer to God alone for our actions.

The strange thing is that those who will not tolerate the smallest deviation from their standard of Christian faith and ethics often end up endorsing schisms and divisions within the church which make far greater havoc of the unity of believers than the original differences ever made. Furthermore, those who allow no deviations from their standards on the grounds that they are keeping the church pure and keeping sin out frequently end up by provoking far greater sin than the small social sins they fear so much. Hear Jesus' terrible words about this: ". . . anyone who looks down on his brother as a lost soul is himself heading straight for the fire of destruction" (Matt. 5:22). We have only to recall the ugly story of the religious wars of the past four centuries to realize that the church has suffered far more from internecine vindictiveness than we like to remember.

It is relevant to us now to look at past history and present dangers because we are always on the verge of becoming judgmental toward others—or else of becoming such squashy Christians that we have no convictions at all. We must find a middle ground to stand on.

That happy middle ground, a place which allows us the utmost commitment to our own convictions and still permits us to respect and honor the convictions of those who differ from us, makes for good friendships *and* for friendship within families. More and more I realize that much of life is spent in building bridges, and that relationships are more important than winning arguments.

It was fairly easy for Russ and me to accept new ideas and ways of thinking on the part of our children, since neither of us had as much education as we were able to give them. We had both read widely, even avidly; reading as a pleasure has always been *the* big "thing" in our family. Still, there were large gaps in our education and we knew it. Sometimes, in discussing philosophy or history, or that fascinating combination of subjects which we call "trying to understand people," we found we didn't agree with what Darrell or Donna said. Not at all! There were some heated discussions, warmed not by anger, but by passionate convictions. We all enjoyed it, and I think—in the long run—we all modified each other's thinking.

Conversation, like reading, has always been our family activity. Others may have played games; we talked. Others may have watched sports; we talked. No doubt we have missed a great deal (our friends tell us so) in not being avid sports fans, but then, conversation had all the fascination of a sport to us.

More and more, as Darrell and Donna brought their friends home for dinner, we found ourselves drawn into their world; and that is a great privilege. It ought not to be abused or trampled on. We discovered that the essential quality we *must* have in order to keep the bridge between the generations in good repair is that of being a good listener. I mean really listening, not simply waiting for the other to stop speaking so I can begin; listening in the sense Jesus meant when he said, as he so often did, "He who has ears to hear, let him hear."

Listening in this sense means, first of all, that we take seriously the person who is speaking—his intelligence and ability to think—that we do not discount his opinions as being, "merely the reflection of a phase," or, "that's just the way all you young folks think these days." It means considering the idea being expressed, and replying seriously; not dodging the issue by such cant as, "When you're as old as I am, you'll know . . ." and so forth.

This kind of listening also demands on the part of a person conversing with someone younger or less knowledgeable a special graciousness. It means that if I have experience and knowledge which my friends or children do not have, I do not use it like a weapon. Sometimes demolishing an argument can also demolish a relationship; far better, and far more Christian, to be gentle about imposing one's superior (we like to think) point of view on others. They may not be ready for it. And, of course, there's always the lurking possibility that experience and knowledge nonetheless, there's new information that makes *my* point of view invalid.

The entire subject of differences we humans must accept—and surmount—in order to get along with one another could be wrapped up by reminding ourselves that in the early church only one confession was necessary to be accepted into the fellowship of believers: "Jesus is Lord." It is right and necessary and good that we grow both spiritually and intellectually; and growth leads to our having opinions. However right our opinions may turn out to be in the clear light of eternity, if we let them divide us from each other, especially from other Christians and from our friends and our families, we have used them wrongly.

I have found the New Testament to be full of solid statements about our faith, statements which give me a base to stand on. One of them is, I believe, that I am required by God to honor the human dignity of others. That means that I listen to them seriously, consider their thinking, and then, if I do not agree, I say so without rejecting them as responsible persons or as Christians. It isn't disagreement that divides, it is rejection.

There will always be issues, some major and some minor, on which Christians will disagree. Since none of us is infallible, we owe each other that debt of love Paul talked about. "Love hurts nobody," Paul said. "Why, then, criticize your brother's actions, why try to make him look small? We shall all be judged one day, not by each other's standards or even our own, but by the judgment of God."

XIII
THE
CIRCLE
WIDENS

IF ALL there is to friendship is shop talk, delightful as that
is at times, life can be deadly.

We all know groups of people who have chosen to live
in a small circle. Their friends are in the same business or
profession. The world they live in is a very tiny world,
bounded by the limits of their field of endeavor. That is a
kind of segregation, self-imposed and just as confining as any
other kind of segregation.

One woman I know always dismisses the opinions of those
she doesn't agree with by saying, "Of course he'd say
that—he's a doctor!" Or, "Well, naturally that's what *she'd*

think—she's English, you know." Sometimes, when there is no handy category to stuff someone in, she simply sniffs and says, "Men!" No one is ever listened to seriously by this person. You can almost see the file cards flipping in her mind as she prepares to pop open a slot to receive anyone who is *different* in any way from her standards. She is a very dull woman.

The penalty for being provincial *is* dullness. On the other hand, the price of learning about our world and the diverse people and cultures in it is a willingness to be uncomfortable. Once in discussing the difficulties some college men and women were undergoing in their European travels my son said, "All learning is painful." I have discovered that is very true indeed. It's much more comfortable to decide on a point of view, or a mode of living, and shut out everything that doesn't fit—or dismiss it as being foolish, wrong or misguided.

Life itself, however, is change. The very process of growing older and acquiring new experiences and new insights ought to help us to widen our horizons.

We will, hopefully, acquire some fresh ways of looking at life. We will, almost certainly, be tempted to crystallize our thinking in some areas because it's more comfortable to do so. The tendency to settle down into a little rut, along which we are proceeding at the same pace as our friends, is very strong.

Life needn't be like that, although it takes a genuine effort to see that we get out of our particular ghetto. My husband and I found that we were shaken out of our rut by our children. They brought their friends and their thinking into our lives and the result was very good. We were forced to be aware, and to be sympathetic (though not always in agreement) with much younger people than ourselves. Some of those whom we first met through Darrell and Donna became, in time, our own friends, quite independent of the relationship with our children.

Among my closest friends are people whom I met when they were in the College Department at church when Darrell was. The difference in our ages has been unimportant in our relationship. Darrell and Donna were the bridge between age groups. Some of my friends' children have become very dear to me, not just because of my relationship with their parents, but because we now have a relationship of our own. To my great delight, my own children are also building friendships with *my* friends, the mothers and fathers of their contemporaries—and they don't need me any more as a link. Donna and Mike are interested in Opal and John quite independently of me. John and Mike talk cameras, and guns, and politics and business not as two men thrust into a relationship because of the ties I have with the Hughes—but because they are developing their own friendship.

By taking part in the women's work at my church, I made friends who were neither in my age group, nor in my social group. Like everyone else, I had found it much easier to stay within the safe confines of my own group, the people Russ and I had come to know in our class at church. We were roughly the same age, at the same point in life, with children at the same stage of development. I assumed a part in the women's work of our church reluctantly, out of a sense of duty, but with no real desire to participate. Yet from the women's work have come some of my most helpful experiences and many of my dearest friends.

Today, those very friends mean more than ever. Again and again Russ and I discovered that keeping ourselves open to new possibilities of friendship brought wider horizons to life. Acquiring new friends does something else, something unexpected—it deepens and strengthens the bonds we have with old friends. Unlike refrigerators and automobiles and all the other mechanical contrivances with built-in obsolescence, new friends don't make the old ones look shabby by comparison—they enhance and deepen relationships that are already strong. I don't know why this is, or how it works—but it does.

Our circle of friends enlarged, and our lives enlarged too as we came to know people in different professions, different businesses, and with different views on contemporary situations. The only thing we had in common was our Christian faith—and it was enough.

We began to feel very strongly, however, that we didn't want to be limited even by our faith. We wanted to be "in the world" as Christ was in the world, to be meeting people and making friends outside the church. We had no motive for making friends outside our faith such as witnessing to them, or being a sort of professional or semi-professional evangelist, using social occasions to talk to people about Christ. We simply felt that we ought not to be in any kind of ghetto, not even a Christian ghetto.

Some of our richest and deepest friendships have come about because we got to know people other than those in our own particular church or religious section. It is my conviction that we were intended by Jesus Christ to be his people in the world in a multitude of ways: by being in our essential selves Christ's men and women; by behaving in a manner consistent with our faith; and finally, by speaking of our faith at the right time, in the right way, with as much consideration for the sensitivities of others as is possible.

What he wants is the kind of commitment to him that makes us real, honest, transparent persons who look at others with clear eyes. We must see them as real people, not as objects to practice our piety on. The friendships we form must be real friendships, taking into account the fact that every single person created is unique in the eyes of God, and worthy of our deeply serious consideration. Some people we will never know more than casually, some we will be better acquainted with, and some will become good friends.

Friendship cannot exist where there is no real respect. Therefore, when we respect another's convictions and beliefs, we do not lightly brush them aside, though we may disagree. After all, it is not up to any of us, however spiritual or however practiced at conveying our faith in words, to win people to Christ. That is God's business; we are merely here for his use. How he conveys his message to the world depends on him. Some of us speak more readily and glibly than others. All of us are used by him one way or another.

I am really making a passionate plea for taking friendship seriously, and for being the kind of people whose lives are good evidence for God. This relieves us of the necessity to convince everyone of our particular point of view, but it obligates us to *be*—always and without ceasing—Christ's people.

I know, when I meet and make friends of people who aren't Christian, that God loves them more than I do. I will speak as persuasively as I can, if the occasion is right; but I will not cheapen the gospel by sliding into what is nothing more than a canned "sales pitch" regardless of time or place.

Having come to know a number of Christians whose theology is not exactly like mine, I am beginning—just beginning—to have some appreciation of the *bigness* of God, and the expansiveness of his grace. His love includes all of us, even if in our mistaken and tragic smallness of mind we shut each other out because of differences in our theologies.

Even though astigmatic Christians may be blind to the possibilities for enriching their lives through friendship with those of diverse tastes, opinions and viewpoints, God does not shut them out. If it were up to me, or up to you, I suspect we would say, "So he doesn't like My children whose liturgy and church form are different from his? Well, then, let him get along without Me as well as he can; love Me, love My children." No, it sometimes seems to me we put our Lord in the unenviable position of a loving parent trying to reconcile his quarreling children. He will not take sides, and he will not abandon even the most spiteful of his erring family.

Two of my very best friends, Bud and Toi Russell, are devout Catholics. We have a strong bond of unity in our mutual love for Christ, and our mutual commitment to his way of life. We don't get together and talk about our differences (although at times, and in certain groups, where such discussion can be constructive, we do). We talk about what binds us together.

At the time Russ became ill with leukemia, Bud—who had been a partner in Russ's business and then gone on to other pursuits—handled the sale of the practice. He gave unstintingly of his time and interest and did the very best for us that anyone could have done, purely out of friendship and Christian love. Everything about our friendship, which has continued to grow since Russ's death, has been rewarding and enriching to me. They strengthen me, they give me encouragement. How poor I would be if I shut out all such friendships on the basis that I must know only those whose viewpoint coincides in all details with mine!

Specialization is necessary for people working in areas where the field of knowledge demands that some people know a lot about a small part of it in order that the whole may be comprehended. But specialization is a bad thing when we apply it indiscriminately to our lives. Most of us need to know a little about a lot of things. We have to keep house, or manage a job, drive a car, cook, serve on committees, be friends—and all at the same time.

In the area of friendship, to specialize is deadly. There, freedom and integration will bring us the incredibly rich rewards of insights into other worlds than ours. As we make new friends we will be doing exactly what our Lord commanded us. After telling his listeners that the greatest commandment was to love God wholly, he said, "And there is a second like it: 'Thou shalt love thy neighbor as thyself.'"

In this life we have a lot of neighbors. Though we won't always agree with them, our part is to love and accept, and to be what God wants us to be. He does the rest; sometimes through us, sometimes not. The important thing is that we *be* the kind of people who make the gospel believable, and attractive. We are called to be neighbors and friends, not to do a job. That implies to me liking and enjoyment, and I'm glad. There is a certain grimness in the concept of the Christian life as a job to be done—a concept which doesn't have quite the New Testament flavor about it. I *like* people—how wonderful it is that the world offers such a fascinating variety!

XIV
THE BEST
AND
THE WORST
OF TIMES

MY MOTHER was the sort of person you were happy to see coming to your front door. She wasn't cloyingly sweet, but she maintained a keen interest in life until the day of her death, and she seldom complained. She had had enough trouble in her life, however, to justify some complaint—married at eighteen, her young husband was killed six months later, leaving her pregnant. She lost the baby, found herself unable to go back home as a dutiful daughter and became a teacher. At thirty she married my father and had three children. Just as we were getting to the most expensive stage of our growth, the depression arrived and the family had some lean years.

The Many Faces Of Friendship

She lost her second child, my brother Russell, in an automobile accident when he had been married less than a year. She suffered painfully and silently for years with crippling arthritis, but always regarded it as an annoyance to be somehow surmounted because there were so many interesting things to do. Her Christianity was evident more in the brisk, matter-of-fact way she viewed her life than in introspection or spiritual soul searchings.

Another woman I knew quite well had suffered some trouble in life and always expected more momentarily. She looked as if she were anticipating bad news and spoke in a failing tone of voice. I used to prepare myself to see her by determining to remain cheerful, but as our conversation wore on, the resolve to bring her spirits up by maintaining my own usually dwindled away and was replaced by an irritated fatigue. These two women typify two opposing views of life. Both were Christians, but I believe my mother enjoyed her faith more.

It is possible (with the evidence of history and our own experience) to conclude, as my pessimist friend had, that life is a series of disturbances ranging from minor annoyances to shattering tragedies; against these, we do the best we can to keep our balance and get some happiness along the way. The non-Christian existentialists who hold this world-view are legion. The astonishing thing is that so many Christians, although they say they trust in the ultimate goodness of God, live their lives as though expecting the worst.

Granted, there are tragedies in life; there are cataclysmic events which wrench one's life out of context; there are daily frustrations with which we must deal. For some people, these troubles, either small or large, occupy such a great part of their thinking that they have no time left to consider the good in life. Yet if we were truly objective, we would conclude, with my mother, that there is more good in life than sorrow. How we regard the good and bad times of life will largely depend on our perspective. The Christian faith has always looked toward a magnificent future. The most extravagant symbolism the writer of Revelation could use was hardly adequate to describe the heavenly city which is our destination. Yet the stories of heaven do not blind us to the realities of today. Paul was not indulging in a flight of fancy or a pious wish, or trying to gloss over unpleasant facts when he wrote: "We are handicapped on all sides, but we are never frustrated; we are puzzled, but never in despair. We are persecuted, but we never have to stand it alone; we may be knocked down but we are never knocked out!"

This was Paul's view of the troubles that constantly beset him; he admitted their power, but they never defeated him. As a realist he had to portray life as it is. For the Christian that means, as Paul said, that "the outward man does indeed suffer wear and tear, but every day the inward man receives fresh strength. These little troubles (which are really so transitory) are winning for us a permanent, glorious and solid reward out of all proportion to our pain. For we are looking all the time not at the visible things but at the invisible. The visible things are transitory; it is the invisible things that are really permanent."

You see the viewpoint Paul lived by? He saw life as a journey toward a glorious goal. The way may be over a chasm, along a precipice, rocky at times, but it has a solidity, a firmness under it; we walk a road that is strong and unshakable, and there is support when we need it. The road under our feet is the truth of the gospel. Jesus compared our obedience to that truth to a foundation that stands through anything because it is built upon a rock.

When we are going through a dangerous patch there is a certain strength in simply going on. To stand still would be to risk complete collapse. There is solace and reinforcement in the structure of life which goes on regardless of disaster. The jobs that demand our attention, the responsibilities we must still carry, the daily duties that have to be taken care of—these are part of the continuity of life which form a support when the going is tough, part of the good things of life.

The other—and equally important—help comes from our friends. They give us support when we need it simply by being there; they don't have to preach, or quote Bible verses, or philosophize, or even express their sympathy in words. They help because they are there. They may often give concrete expression of their friendship; they bring food when there is sickness or death, do the ironing, clean the house, give anonymous gifts of money, and put themselves to great inconvenience to run errands and carry out commissions.

What makes all these "good deeds" so heartwarming, however, is not that they are good deeds, but that they are done out of friendship, often quietly and even surreptitiously. Not paraded for all to see and admire, they are the by-products of genuine friendship. No doubt those who do such things, if asked about their good deeds would reply with some surprise, "*Good* deed? Good heavens, no, it's what anyone would do—why, old Joe is a friend of mine!" The fact that old Joe is a friend is all that matters. It is just that sort of friendship which has the flavor of heaven about it; most of its goodness lies in its unself-consciousness.

These past few years have confirmed my belief that Paul's view of life is the true one, that the planks I walk on are dependable and the supports on either side will hold me up.

I do not want to gloss over the distresses that are common to us all. Life can become, at times, a battlefield. All this is taken into account, quite matter-of-factly, by the writers of the New Testament, as we have seen.

As a Christian I believe we have every right, indeed are compelled both by logic and experience, to view life not as a series of disasters of varying degrees but as a journey: though from time to time it is *beset by troubles,* it is also lightened and made merry by much goodness and pleasure. Neither trouble nor pleasure cancels the other out, and there are innumerable instances of both. The particular pleasure—and goodness—that this book is about is that which friends give us.

The last five years of Russ's life were the best years we had together. After so long a time of stress because of illness, financial hardships, and other assorted troubles, we entered a smooth, untroubled period of life. By untroubled I don't mean that the surface of life was never ruffled by friction between us. We were both strong-minded people, and we had some *very* interesting fights. They cleared the air, and kept the channels of communication open. (I have often wondered about people who say they never ever have an argument: is it because neither one has opinions strong or definite enough to stand up for? or one or the other always gives in to keep the peace? or they are not telling the truth?)

With Darrell studying for a Ph.D. in Hamburg, Germany, and coming home once a year or so, we were finding our horizons broadened to include more of the world than we had known before. We also made several trips abroad. Donna, in college, kept us entertained with the droll wit that had manifested itself almost with her first words. Life was interesting, full of discoveries about our children, our friends, and the world. Russ's business was going very well and the years ahead promised even more prosperity.

More and more we cherished the relationships that had grown stronger with the years. We had been through many troubled times with our friends, had come to know one another intimately. There was a solid ground of understanding about such friendships which imparted a relaxed, easy quality to our time together; no need to worry if one spoke hastily, or somewhat too strongly at times—we were judged not by our occasional lapses from good sense, but by the total relationship.

We never found in any of those who had become so close to us the slightest tendency to build any walls around us, or to become a clique. All of us were reaching out for new relationships. We used to talk about our conviction that any friendship, if it becomes exclusive, will lose its vitality. How thankful I am that none of our friends ever expected us to be totally absorbed in them; they knew that the ability to give oneself in friendship is a quality, not a quantity, and that there is never a point at which one says, "There. That's enough, I have all the friends I need."

Where sexual love is exclusive, friendship is inclusive. It is somewhat like the links of a chain: one link connects to another. That's the way we came to know some of the people who made a great difference to our lives.

When Jack and Althea Franck introduced us to Dr. and Mrs. William Van Valin and Dr. and Mrs. Raymond Cramer all of us found our appreciation of each other expanding geometrically. Russ and Bill Van Valin experienced instant rapport, as Pauli and I did, and we found our relationship growing rapidly. Because Bill and Russ had much the same background, they were very close to each other; there was a kind of wordless empathy between them. The remarkable thing about such a new relationship is that it always adds a dimension to the friendships one already has. Russ and Jack Franck were closer because Bill was a friend of both.

We had also met Floyd and Harriett Thatcher through the Cramers, and they made an astonishing difference in our lives, because Floyd, who was President of Cowman Publications, was responsible for my first serious attempt at writing. Without his encouragement—and goading—I might have given the project up; but he and Russ between them kept me at it.

The four of us grew to be very close friends indeed, and had known each other for at least four years before we discovered quite by accident that we had all been in the same school at the same time, in Ventura. We had doubtless passed one another in the corridors many times. Would we have responded then, as we did years later, to each other? I think not. There is, as the writer of Ecclesiastes wrote centuries ago, a time for everything; and the timing of our friendship was just right. We were ready for the new dimension to life that these relationships brought with them, and we found that life was more stimulating than ever. This kind of new experience confirms my belief that the good things in life far outweigh the troubles.

Of course, there is always the danger, especially in writing a book such as this, that one will stress the difficulties so that the story seems to be all tension, pain and disaster. That is because it is always easier to be detailed (and dramatic) about the times when life is cataclysmic than it is about the happy times. What can one say beyond, "We were happy; days, weeks, months went by, full of small duties and regular jobs, good times with friends and no real troubles."

And yet, those are the days that make up most of our lives,

unless we spend so much time thinking about all the distressing events that we aren't able to appreciate present good. Russ and I did a great deal of talking about "present good." Of course, we were busy; everyone was busy, there is never enough time simply to be together; but that, no doubt will come in heaven. We used to talk with Jack and Althea Franck, whose friendship had been strong through the years, about the brevity of our times together and Jack would usually say, "We ought to take more time just to *be* with our friends."

That's true, of course, but as I look back on those years I remember very vividly the quality of hours spent with them and with Bill and Pauli Van Valin. I remember conversations around many dinner tables; and lazy Sunday afternoons with Helen and Milford Childers, Florence and Stan Colloran, and Opal and John Hughes. These times together made an imprint on my memory—and on Russ's—far greater than the total of the hours spent.

There were other times when Russ was plagued by business irritations, or when things didn't go right at home. I don't dwell on those memories, I remember the happy, rewarding times instead. One must choose which side of life to remember. I know people whose outlook is so embittered and cynical because they have kept all their troubles in the forefront of their thinking that they increase their unhappiness, and repel friendship. We can all sympathize with those in trouble (and Russ and I knew how much that could help), but no one can stand being constantly in the role of a chorus for a Greek tragedy.

Russ said one evening, "You know, I never dreamed when we were first married that we'd be able to do the things we've done, and to experience what we've experienced. I feel we've accomplished the most important job in life just in being able to bring our children up in the faith, to educate them and see them happily married. I never thought I'd go to Europe, or that we'd have the kind of life we have and the friends we have. I sometimes feel that anything more God gives me will be just gravy."

Later that year, when we found he had leukemia, I remembered those words. The philosophy he expressed was true. I believe it now more than ever. After years of serenity and (for the most part) untroubled living, we met again the issue of serious illness, and inevitable death. There was a great difference, however. We had asked all the questions before, and the answers were there. We knew that, however much we enjoyed earthly pleasures, they were not the end for which we lived. We knew that nothing but ultimate joy in the presence of Christ would satisfy our deepest longings. And so we were able to live through the days of Russ's illness and growing weakness with serenity and trust.

My first book for women, *We're Never Alone,* had been published just before Russ's illness. At that time Eugenia Price, a close friend of the Thatchers, sent me a congratulatory telegram. I wrote and thanked her, and she answered. When she got the word that Russ had leukemia, she kept writing—the warmest, most understanding and helpful letters I have ever received. Russ and Genie had their own correspondence, and I received from her just a few weeks ago a letter he had written her, telling of his faith in Christ. Genie became a close friend then, months before we met face to face, and I am constantly astonished at her generosity and sensitivity to people.

During Russ's last months there were moments, of course, when the questions came back and sounded louder in our ears than the answers; but they were only moments. The certainty that death is not the end, but only a way station for a Christian, was not something we deluded ourselves with. It was not a wistful hope that all might turn out well in the end. It was a conviction which gripped us, rather than a position we held to. The difference may sound subtle to one who has never known such a conviction, nor felt the weight of the utterly "other" crowding out all human doubt; but it is a real difference. It is like the sureness we all have of our own identity, our separateness as persons, in contrast to a belief in fairies or elves.

Again, at times when we were oppressed beyond our strength, there were friends at hand to reassure and uphold us. Ruth Green Plowman was a special help during those days. She was working in hematology at the Center for the Health Sciences at U.C.L.A. where Russ's disease was finally diagnosed, and she used to drop by several times a day to chat with him. When I was unsettled by well-meant advice, all of it different, Ruth calmed me by saying, "Just hang tight."

One day, shortly after the diagnosis of leukemia was made and Russ had come home from the hospital, he asked Dick Langford to come and see him. Dick listened while Russ told him how, in spite of his gratitude for things he had been able to accomplish, he felt a sense of frustration at being cut off in the prime of life. After all, there were many things he still wanted to do, and although he was proud of his family he was a very unassuming man about his personal achievements. He hadn't gone to the mission field or been a great preacher, nor did he have the gift of verbalizing his faith easily and quickly when talking to acquaintances. He was definitely *not* a man who "witnessed" at the drop of a hat—or who leaped into a conversational silence with his handy little message. What did his life really add up to?

Dick Langford is not one to give a pat answer, or quickly reel off a passage from the Bible. He talked with Russ about the real issues of the Christian life—about *being*, rather than simply doing. He talked about the importance of living in circumstances like the rest of contemporary society lives in, but as a Christian whose ethics and morals are consistent with Jesus' teaching and the standards of the New Testament rather than "what everyone else does." After an hour or so together, the burden was lifted and Russ was comforted.

We had decided, as soon as we knew what his illness was, that it was better to tell everyone the truth rather than keep up a pretence which would grow more difficult to sustain as time went by. We wanted to live, as much as possible, normal lives, not an invalidish sort of life, and so we did. Russ had sold his practice, an immediate necessity because of his weakness, and was at home. We had devotions together, he read, he visited with the many friends who dropped by constantly. We even had a potluck dinner the Saturday before he died. He was too weak by then to come downstairs, but we all went up to our bedroom after dinner. Helen and Milford Childers were there, Opal and John Hughes, Florence and Stan Colloran and Herman and Dixie Baerer; there were twenty years of friendship between us. We looked at slides taken at long past picnics, when we were all much younger and our children were small. The reminiscences and laughter may have been somewhat subdued, but they were genuine. Such evenings as that were a tremendous help to both Russ and to me. We were living each day and savoring its flavor.

One of the hardest things to endure, for both of us, was the uncertainty of the time he would have, made infinitely more complicated by the fact that early in the summer, before he was ill, we had set Donna's wedding date as December

18th. In November, when the diagnosis was made, we both acted on the assumption that Russ would have an indefinite amount of time ahead; the medication would help; some new discovery would be made—you can imagine how our thoughts ran.

We never considered postponing the wedding or changing the plans, not even after several stays in the hospital to receive blood transfusions, nor in view of his growing weakness. In the back of my mind, however, the possibility of a sudden turn for the worse lurked. I think Donna and I both felt that to change the wedding plans would be to proclaim to Russ that we expected him to die. It was such an unthinkable course of action that it was never an option.

Perhaps someone is thinking at this point, "She hasn't even mentioned prayer. Why not? Doesn't she believe that believing prayer will save the sick man?" Yes, we did believe that God does sometimes heal; we believed that he answers prayers. But then we also knew that the assumption that *all* prayer, if one's faith is right, results in getting what one has asked for, like a card popped out of the weighing machine, was false. Prayer is asking. We ask out of our finiteness, our imperfect knowledge and wills and motives. God answers out of his perfect will for our lives, and the answers are not always in the shape we had expected.

Of course we prayed that God would heal Russ, and Russ believed fervently that he would. He had a definite healing experience just after Thanksgiving when his condition was terminal. After one of the elders of our church, Bob Hunter, prayed with Russ, overnight and without any more blood his blood count jumped five points and he was able to come home from the hospital. That was God working we believed, and he healed Russ. The confusion comes because we always assume that when there has been healing, the person made whole will then die years later of old age. God has his timing, however, and this healing was for a time and a purpose. I do not understand all the facets of what God was doing, of course; I merely know that Russ was able to escort Donna down the aisle on December 18th; that with Darrell and his wife, Linda, home from Germany for the wedding and for Christmas, it was a very radiant time.

One of the great sources of strength for both of us was that our friends were confident as we were that God was in control. Nobody came and exhorted us to "pray a little harder," or, "claim these promises." There was always the possibility that one of the very sophisticated chemotherapies his doctor was using would arrest the progress of the disease. There were infinite possibilities, but they lay in God's hands. We felt that our salvation (I use the word carefully) lay in living every day as if it were all we would have. When you come right down to it, *this* day is all any of us will have—for certain. Tomorrow, whatever plans we have made for it, is not under our control; it is not what God gave us to work with. He gave us *today*.

Not everyone is as blessed as we were in having mature, understanding friends. How very cruel many Christians are, with their prating of "the prayer of faith," and their little speeches about how they *just know God is going to raise you up, dear.* Unintentionally cruel, of course, but inflicting deep wounds nevertheless. There has been so much silliness in the Christian community about the problem of pain and suffering, so much wishful thinking about the whole subject, that most Christians feel very guilty if they are ill. There are times when we must take somewhat the same attitude toward these mistaken believers in the easy, effortless, free-from-all-trouble

Christian life that Jesus showed to Peter. Peter didn't like what Jesus was saying about the cross ahead. When he remonstrated with Jesus, his master turned on him and said, "Out of my way, Satan! . . . You stand right in my path, Peter, when you look at things from man's point of view and not from God's."

And now we have come full circle. We began this chapter by saying that there is more good in life than sorrow, more to rejoice in than to fear. We end it by saying that when sorrow comes, as it does to all men (who are we to escape?) we can, if we trust Christ, accept it as we accept all the pleasant things of life at his hands. After all, as the Bible reminds us, our eventual destination puts this world's best to shame and it would be the height of folly to forget our destination and settle down at some way-station in life.

XV
GOING
ON

AS THEY had been all through Russ's illness, friends were with us to the end. Writers have commented frequently upon the solitariness of life; how all the most important crises of our lives are faced by oneself and that death is the final lonely journey. That is only partly true. Once we belong to Jesus we have his word that we will never be alone again. He said, "I call you friends," and because he met death alone we do not. He is with us, the one inseparable companion.

On this side of that final chasm, however, are the many friends who make our days more bearable. They are, in a sense, "little Christs" to us as they fulfill his command to love one another and bear burdens for each other. The easy flow of conversation each day as people dropped in to chat was not a pretence that everything was normal, or an attempt to push away the inevitability of death. Those who think that we ought to drop everything and concentrate on whatever catastrophe is impending forget that life—daily life with its little comings and goings, its small duties and everyday talk—is the *reality* and death is merely an interruption, or for the Christian a transition, in the process of living.

So having our friends about us helped us to enjoy each day, and when the end came and I was momentarily dazed, they quietly carried me along the procession of necessary duties. Death is nearly always a surprise, even after a long illness when one knows the end is inevitable. I do not think this is because we can't face reality, or aren't "spiritual" enough to be ready for Heaven, but because God put into us a fervent desire for life. Life, in its ultimate sense, means life released from the limitations of time and space, life with Christ in eternity; but that is so removed from our experience that we can conceive of it only in terms we already know, in terms of *this* life, here on earth.

Every Christian, faced with the termination of life here, knows that something better awaits. None of our deepest longings have been fulfilled on earth.

C. S. Lewis, speaking of the wordless longing for something nameless, indescribable, coming to us through music or books or a landscape—likens it to ". . . the scent of a flower we have not found, the echo of a tune we have not heard, news from a country we have never yet visited." He concludes, in the essay, "Weight of Glory," that this longing will only find its fulfillment in heaven. It is a desire which does not negate the life we now have but tells us there is *more* life.

But the clinging to the life we have, the stubborn resistance to death, is our human way of affirming our enthusiasm for life, whether here or there. A healthy regard for this world is, for the Christian, a symbol of our conviction that as God is sovereign here, so he is of eternity. Suicide is not an attempt to plunge, a little early, into eternal life; it is a negation of belief that life is good at all, a denial of both heaven and earth.

And so life went on; for Russ, life in a different dimension; for me, life in a new direction. After twenty-seven years of marriage, of being primarily a wife and a mother, old duties were removed and a new door opened. That is the way God ordains it, if we open our eyes to what he is doing. There never ought to be a complete vacuum in life; we usually put them there ourselves, by refusing to see what comes next.

After the publication of my book, *We're Never Alone,* it seemed evident to me that there was an opportunity to continue writing. So, after a few weeks spent in getting my affairs in order and learning how to handle things that Russ had always taken care of, I started another book. And when that one was finished, I wrote another one—and now this.

It all sounds so simple—first I did one thing, then I did the next. But I could not have done it at all if it had not been for the constant, though unobtrusive, support of my friends. They neither treated me as an emotionally unstrung woman who had to be handled delicately, nor left me on my own. They were just there, as they had always been there. They did not expect me to display either a phony sort of Christian joy (as if what had happened didn't hurt at all) or to grieve publicly. I am one of those people who *has* to be alone to weep. I don't know why, other than that I was forced to keep swallowing my tears long years ago when Russ was drafted during World War II and the children and I were living with my parents. They were not demonstrative people, and would have found it very trying to have me dribbling about the house. At any rate, after Russ's death I found the matter-of-fact acceptance of my friends comforting.

We could even laugh at some of the unconscious humor such situations provoke. I wanted to keep our home, which we loved, and where we had been happy; but *at least* several times each week someone said to me, "Well, Mrs. Guder, and are you going to keep on living all alone in that great big house?" (The house isn't that big, and I *did* keep on living there.) Bob Ringer often greeted me with those very words in such a perfect mimicry of conventional sympathizers that we laughed. Laughter is a healing thing, just as tears are healing; and sometimes I laughed, and sometimes—alone—I cried. But always there were things to be done, and business to be taken care of, and friends near by so that I never felt lonely.

Genie Price wrote often, as only she can write, heartening and practical and humorous and understanding letters. I hadn't yet met her, nor Joyce Blackburn, although by now, after months of correspondence I felt I knew them both. In the fall of that year I spent several weeks with Floyd and Harriett Thatcher in Grand Rapids, and then the three of us drove to St. Simon's Island to see Genie and Joyce. Meeting them face to face was a unique experience. It was an instant recognition of friendship, an acknowledgement of a dimension that was already there. In the years since that time, the friendship has grown deeper and stronger, and Genie has literally pushed me up the ladder as a writer. Each time we are together, I am more aware of the constant procession of good God adds to my life.

It is true the pattern of life has altered. I do different things now than I did when the children were home and Russ came home to dinner every night, but I still have more to do than there is time in which to do it. The same friends Russ and I were close to are dearer to me than ever, and there are new friends. I travel more now than I did before, and have met all kinds of interesting people. Some of them will be old friends, some day, as they are new ones now. When I stay with the Halversons, in Washington, it is like being in my own home, so secure and relaxed is our relationship. When the Thatchers and I are together, we have the same easy relationship we had before. I go out to dinner, I entertain, just as I did before. Opal and I get together as often as we can, just as we did before. These friends, in short, make up the continuity of life which has been disturbed and altered by death. They are, although they don't think of themselves in any such exalted fashion, God's ministers to me as well as to many others; ministers through friendship.

I do not know what waits in the future for me. Most of my hopes are wrapped up in my children: Darrell and Linda, Donna and Michael. For them I pray for good, useful, faithful lives lived in commitment to Jesus Christ; with all the happiness that God gives his children, and with all the integrity and staunch faith one needs in this life.

Looking back, I can see that there has been nothing out of the ordinary in the events of my life. Marriage and children, varying kinds of illness and financial troubles, tension and stress, times of serenity and pleasure, the death of parents and husband and child—all these are the common stuff of life. These are the situations all men and women live through. We do not think them especially worthy of note; no one writes them up in newspaper stories.

And yet, in the everyday lives of ordinary people quite remarkable things are happening underneath, or behind, the commonplace progression of time. We are moving inexorably toward eternity; making, or marring our journey by our own most minute decisions; being helped or hindered by everyone around us. The New Testament is for us, the unexceptional people who are called upon to work out our faith—our radical, uncommon, exceptional faith—in the humdrum affairs of this world.

Very few of us will rise to positions of prominence, or influence the course of history. If we are involved in cataclysmic events (as we well may be) it will be as those caught up in the vortex of such explosions, not as ones whose decisions shake nations.

Because God became one of us in Jesus Christ, he has made all the ordinariness of life important, and all the insignificant matters of personal relationships eternally significant. We really *do* make irrevocable imprints on each other, for good or for ill. Friendship, that quiet, unspectacular, usually unsung and unheroic affinity between human beings, is the vehicle of many of these imprints. In the light of the real world beyond our time-space world, therefore, friendship may loom larger than any persuasion of rhetoric or any display of power.

Trumpets are sounded for great or solemn events here: the advance of armies, the return of the victors, or solemn ceremonies; but I think it quite probable that, though we do not hear them, trumpets are sounding all the time in heaven for the unremarked words and deeds of people we know.

Russ had a gift for friendship. He was a quiet man, (no trumpets before him) but he looked at every man he met, in business or any other way, as a man with whom friendship might be possible. No one was ever, "merely a client," or a business account. Because he was also a man of integrity, his friendship for others was accompanied by absolute honesty.

When it came to the marker for his grave, Darrell, Donna and I were of one mind—we wanted a quotation from Bunyan's, *Pilgrim's Progress.* There is a paragraph that tells about how, after a long journey, Mr. Valiant-for-Truth was sent for; eternity waited for him, but first he must cross the river. As he crossed he could be heard quoting Paul's words from I Corinthians 15, "Death, where is thy sting?" and, "Grave, where is thy victory?"

We put on the marker the last sentence of that paragraph from Bunyan: "So he passed over, and all the trumpets sounded for him on the other side."

The trumpets will sound for all of us eventually—all who cling to Christ, however imperfectly and ignorantly. But I am sure they are sounding now, if we could only hear them, for the countless numbers of quiet people who go about every day just being someone's friend.

For further reading—

DELIVER US FROM FEAR. By Eileen Guder. About that many-headed monster, fear: the fear of becoming involved; the fear of change; the fear of rejection; the fear of failure; the fear of death. The author suggests biblical, practical ways of looking our fears in the face, calling them by name, describing what they do to us, and putting the spiritual remedy—faith—to work. #80415 (hardback)

THE NAKED I: SEEKING GOD AND FINDING IDENTITY. By Eileen Guder. "The world is full of people trying to enjoy the rewards of several roles, while avoiding the obligation of any of them." A guide for all of us caught in the paradox of human frustrations on one hand and the hope of participation with God on the other. #98072 (quality paperback).

YES IS A WORLD. By James W. Angell. A rousing welcome into the life of affirmation. This hope-filled book includes chapters titled: Man Is Born with Rainbows in His Heart; Not the Postponed Life; Transcendence Is a Kiss on the Nose; Dancing on a Battlefield. #80387 (hardback).

EIGHTH DAY OF CREATION. By Elizabeth O'Connor. The human spirit's infinite capacity for creativity; how anyone can discover his life's purpose. Where others see danger and failure, Elizabeth O'Connor sees opportunity, the possibility of a renaissance of compassion, love, and spiritual fulfillment. #80260 (hardback).

COME TO THE PARTY. By Karl A. Olsson. An invitation to a celebration of life. Describes the author's pilgrimage from the world of academe to a life-style of honest relationships and real humanity. Tells how you can recognize and affirm your own spiritual gifts and the gifts of others as an indispensable part of living. #80296 (hardback); #98001 (quality paperback).

ALL YOU LONELY PEOPLE/ALL YOU LOVELY PEOPLE. By John Killinger. How often do you admit your loneliness or find escape from its crippling frustration? The author recalls meetings, incidents, confrontations and emotions to demonstrate how people can share each other's lives. Perceptive insights into the very essence of sharing relationships. #80315 (hardback).

TO KISS THE JOY. By Robert A. Raines. Reveals the author's deep awareness of the painfulness of growth; the yearning for the comfort of yesterday; the sense of fear when faith is threatened. Urges the reader to live boldly, immediately; to live in unison with his dreams, daring to risk much. #80324 (hardback)

ENJOY THE JOURNEY. By Lionel A. Whiston. Accepting the fact that God loves us in spite of our failures, understanding our fellow man, and facing up to moral responsibility are just a few of the keys to a fuller spiritual life which the author explains and analyzes in this helpful book. #80250 (hardback).

140